Contents

Publisher's Introduction		5
Walk 1	RUNNYMEDE AND COOPER'S HILL	7
Walk 2	VIRGINIA WATER IN WINDSOR GREAT PARK	11
Walk 3	ETON: WITH BOVENEY AND DORNEY COMMON	17
Walk 4	ASCOT - THROUGH WINDSOR FOREST AND THE CROWN ESTATE	23
Walk 5	THE HAUNT OF HIGHWAYMEN: MAIDENHEAD THICKET	27
Walk 6	COOKHAM AND BOURNE END	33
Walk 7	THE THAMES AT HURLEY	39
Walk 8	WOKINGHAM TO CROWTHORNE VIA GORRICK PLANTATION	45
Walk 9	KNOWL HILL AND WALTHAM ST LAWRENCE	53
Walk 10	HENLEY AND REMENHAM	59

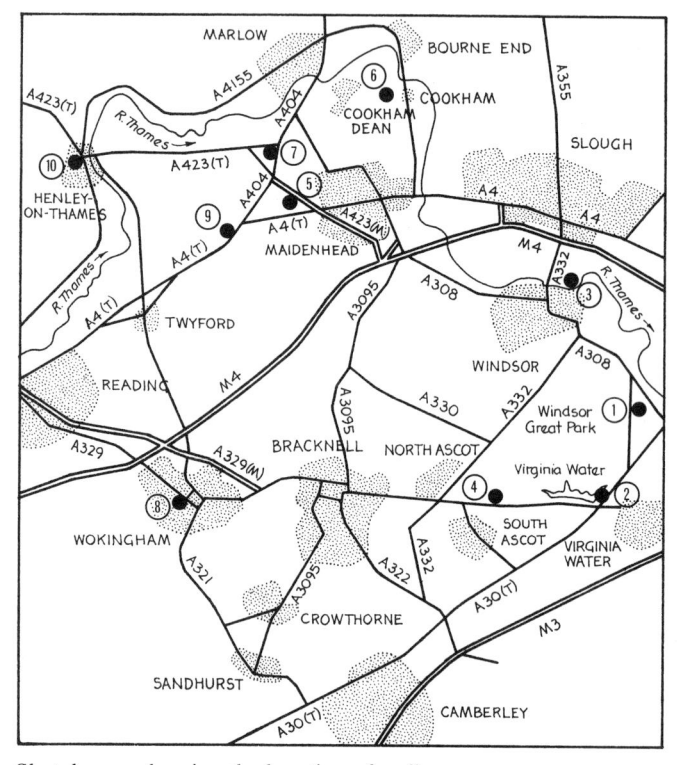

Sketch map showing the location of walks.

WALKS IN EAST BERKSHIRE
Ten Country Rambles near Reading, Maidenhead, Windsor and Wokingham

Mick Tapp

With Historical Notes

COUNTRYSIDE BOOKS
NEWBURY, BERKSHIRE

First Published 1984
© Mick Tapp 1984

All rights reserved. No reproduction
permitted without the prior permission
of the publishers:
COUNTRYSIDE BOOKS
3 Catherine Road
Newbury Berkshire
ISBN 0 905392 28 0

Designed by Mon Mohan
Sketch maps by David Thelwell
Cover photograph of Quarry Wood, Bisham,
taken by the author
Produced through MRM (Print Consultants) Ltd., Baughurst, Hants.
Printed in England by Riverside Press (Reading)

Publisher's Introduction

The walks in this book have been chosen because they offer a good variety of country scenery; riverside, lakeside, forest, heathland, meadow and parkland, all of it a haven of greenery and a welcome escape from the noise and bustle of urban life. At the same time they are leisurely enjoyable affairs that can each be completed in a few hours.

All of them are circular and their starting points have space for car parking. Public transport is shown where it is available.

For those who like to break their walk for refreshment the names of good pubs and places serving tea along or near the routes are mentioned.

The Historical Notes are designed to provided basic information about the places of interest along the route, and will be found at the end of each chapter.

The sketch map that accompanies each walk is designed to guide walkers to the starting point and give a simple but accurate idea of the route to be taken. For those who like the benefit of detailed maps the relevant Ordnance Survey 1:50,000 series sheet is recommended.

The walks are all along public footpaths and highways, but bear in mind that deviation orders may be made from time to time. Please also remember the Country Code and make sure gates are not left open nor any farm animals disturbed.

No special equipment is needed to enjoy the countryside on foot, but do wear a stout pair of shoes and remember that at least one muddy patch is likely even on the sunniest day.

Nicholas Battle

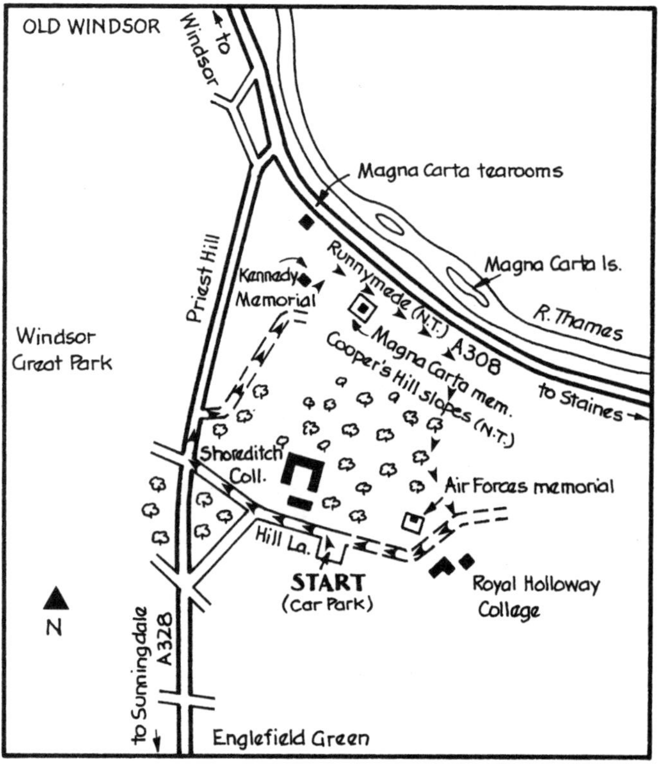

OLD WINDSOR
to Windsor
Magna Carta tearooms
Kennedy Memorial
Runnymede (N.T.)
Magna Carta Is.
R. Thames
Priest Hill
Windsor Great Park
A308
Magna Carta mem.
Cooper's Hill slopes (N.T.)
to Staines
Shoreditch Coll.
Air Forces memorial
Hill La.
START
(Car Park)
Royal Holloway College
N
to Sunningdale
A328
Englefield Green

WALK ONE

Runnymede and Cooper's Hill

Introduction: This is a short walk around the beautiful wooded slopes of Cooper's Hill and level, open Runnymede that lies below them. The route, although short, is crammed with points of interest along the way. It visits a memorial to the late President Kennedy; the meadow, Runnymede, where Magna Carta was signed 750 years ago and the modern Air Forces Memorial. There are absorbing views from Cooper's Hill and the scenery along the whole of the route is very attractive. It is easy to see why Sir John Denham was inspired to write of it in his poem, 'Cooper's Hill'. It was published in 1643 and is said to be the first recorded poem written to extol the attractions of a local beauty spot. The walk is not difficult but after extremely wet periods the ground at the foot of Cooper's Hill can hold water.

Distance: The route is 2¼ miles long and will take about 1¼ hours to walk. You can allow at least as much time again for sightseeing along the way.

Refreshments: There is a refreshment kiosk in the car park where the walk begins and Magna Carta Tearooms are situated at the edge of Runnymede nearly half way round the circuit. They are both open during the summer months only.

How to get there: Head towards Englefield Green. It lies within a triangle formed by Windsor, Staines and Sunningdale. When near the village follow signs towards the Air Forces Memorial. Go into Cooper's Hill Lane and park in a car park on the right that is provided for visitors to the Memorial.

WALK ONE

The walk: Go out from the car park to Cooper's Hill Lane and turn left along it. It is a pleasant leafy lane that goes for ½ mile to a 'T' junction. Turn right where it is signed St Judes Road and begin to go down Priest Hill (see notes). This downhill stretch is lined on each side with oakwoods. There is a long forward view across the Thames Valley and Datchet Reservoir.

300 yards after turning out of Cooper's Hill Lane and just where the wood on the right ends, turn into a dark narrow lane that leads off to the right. It is enclosed by lofty oaks and chestnuts and is named Oak Lane. Go along the lane. It swings to the left and heads downhill with Shoreditch College sports fields along the right-hand side. At the end of the sports field the lane turns to the right. Ignore this turn and continue the forward direction along a footpath. It goes between trees for about 300 yards and then emerges into the open once more.

The path leads to a large white block of stone inscribed to the memory of the late John F. Kennedy, President of the U.S.A. (see notes). A pleasant cobblestone path with steps leads on downhill, through trees, to a wooden kissing gate at the bottom of the slope. Go through the gate to a broad level meadow. This is Runnymede, renowned throughout the world as the place where the seeds of democracy were sown when King John signed Magna Carta here nearly eight centuries ago.

Ahead, across the meadow, is a busy road and the River Thames and Magna Carta Island. Half-left, 400 yards across the meadow are two identical single storey lodges; one each side of the road where it enters Runnymede (see notes). The left-hand one houses the Magna Carta Tearooms. Just beyond the other is a boathouse from where river trips are run in summer.

Continue the walk by turning right after passing through the kissing gate. Walk along the edge of the meadow for 300 yards to where a gate on the right-hand side leads to a railed-off area with a stone monument under a canopy at its centre. This is the monument erected to commemorate the signing of Magna Carta (see notes).

Return from the enclosure with the Magna Carta monument to the open meadow. Turn right. A wire fence crosses the meadow from the monument's enclosure to the road but a gap thirty paces out from the enclosure has been left to allow walkers through. Continue along the edge of the meadow under the beautiful slopes of Cooper's Hill. Follow alongside the hedge and fence for ¼ mile to where a gap gives access to a footpath that goes off to the right, away from the meadow. This path winds between hedges and fences towards the wooded hillslope in front.

Go into the wood and up the slope. The path follows the line of a fence a dozen yards away at the right-hand edge of the wood. 150 yards into the wood the path veers to the left and angles across the slope which becomes steadily steeper. The path is well used and easily followed. Its surface is clay and can become slippery in wet weather. The wood is owned by the National Trust and is very beautiful to walk through. If you are quiet you will see grey squirrels leaping lightly from branch to branch and hear woodland birds calling from the foliage above. The path passes under the white stone Air Forces Memorial perched high on the top edge of the hill. It then comes out to a stony track at the edge of the wood.

Turn right and walk along this track. It goes by Kingswood Hall, part of Royal Holloway College, and acquires a made-up surface. After 200 yards turn right into Cooper's Hill Lane. On the right-hand side are the well-kept grounds that surround the Air Forces Memorial. The entrance is 70 yards along the lane. The memorial is a most beautiful and tranquil building set in equally beautiful and tranquil grounds (see notes). The views from its tower are particularly memorable. They take in Heathrow Airport, the Thames, Runnymede and Windsor.

Return from the Air Forces Memorial to Cooper's Hill Lane. Turn right and go along the tree-lined road for 250 yards to the car-park on the left-hand side where the walk began.

Runnymede - Historical Notes

Priest Hill: In a meadow near here was fought the last recorded fatal duel in England. In 1845 two Frenchmen fought until one was mortally wounded. The survivor was charged with murder, stood trial and was acquitted.

Kennedy Memorial: This large block of Portland stone was erected to the memory of John F. Kennedy, popular President of the U.S.A. who was assassinated in 1963. The monument was set up here in 1965. It stands upon an acre of ground that was given by the people of Britain to the people of America as a tribute to their former President.

WALK ONE

Runnymede: It was here that the Barons and the Church secured the Royal Seal to a greater charter (Magna Carta) which guaranteed basic freedoms and justice to all. It took place at a meeting between King John and the Barons in the summer of 1215. The king rode out from Windsor Castle and the Barons from their encampment at Staines. The undertakings given by the king at this great confrontation have been adhered to ever since. Runnymede is still an unspoilt open meadow. It has not been built on although there was a racecourse here for about a hundred years until 1886. This historic meadow is now owned by the National Trust. It was given in memory of the father of the first Lord Fairhaven in 1931. Lutyens designed the lodges that mark its limits where the road goes in and out. It now draws large numbers of visitors, and car parks are provided for them near the river. It is freely open at all times.

Magna Carta Monument: This memorial was raised by the American Bar Association and paid for by contributions from its 900 members. It was set up here in 1957. By the gate to its enclosure is a showcase containing a facsimile of Magna Carta and a translation of it.

Air Forces Memorial: This war memorial was built by and is maintained by the Commonwealth War Graves Commission. It is a beautiful white stone building set around the four sides of an open courtyard. Each side is about fory paces long. It was unveiled by the Queen in 1953 and records the names of 20,000 airmen and women of Commonwealth Air Forces who died during the Second World War in Britain and in northern and western Europe and who have no other known grave. The names of those remembered are carved in the stonework in letters about an inch high. They are in endless columns around the walls of the cloisters. A register is available to check whether the name of a friend or relation is recorded here. The memorial is open from 9am daily (10am Sundays) until 8pm except in winter when it is closed at dusk.

WALK TWO

Virginia Water in Windsor Great Park

Introduction: Virginia Water is a large ornamental lake that straddles the Berkshire/Surrey border close to Virginia Water village. It is set in beautifully landscaped parkland in the south-east corner of Windsor Great Park and forms part of the Crown Estate. The puplic are admitted freely during daylight hours and the paths, car parks (coin operated barriers) and other facilities are all first-class. This walk makes a full circuit of the lake and visits several places of interest along the way. The route offers gentle walking in exceptionally beautiful surroundings.

Distance: This walk is about 4½ miles in length and will take about 2 hours to complete. The paths are so good that a child's push-chair can be taken around without difficulty.

Refreshments: At weekends and other popular times a mobile refreshments stall operates in the car park. The Wheatsheaf Hotel, beside the A.30, 150 yards from the car park entrance offers full restaurant facilities. The Seven Stars public house on the A.329 just 150 yards from the park entrance at Blacknest provides traditional pub fare. Full restaurant service can be had at the Belvedere Arms, a few steps on from the Seven Stars.

How to get there: Make your way to the car park at the entrance to Virginia Water beside the A.30 trunk road between Staines and Sunningdale. It is easily found just a short way from the entrance to Wentworth Golf Club and the well-known Wheatsheaf Hotel.

The walk: Go away from the main road and through a wooden gate at the back of the car park. 100 yards of open woodland sepa-

WALK TWO

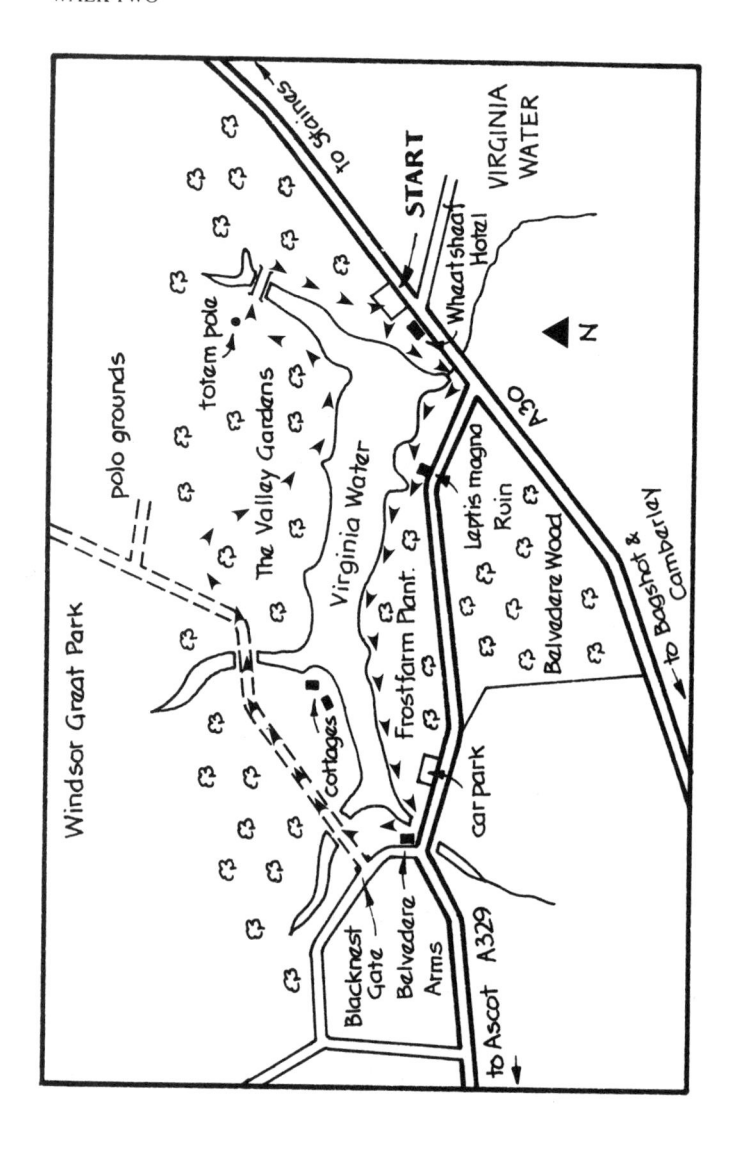

VIRGINIA WATER

rate you from the shore of Virginia Water. Its glinting surface can already be seen between the trees. At the water's edge turn left along a well-made path. There is a long clear view up the lake from here. It is a beautiful clear expanse of water surrounded by gently upsloping woods and with secluded bays and creeks going off on each side, (see notes).

After 300 yards leave the lakeside path by turning left by a cluster of big brown boulders. Follow a footpath for 25 yards downhill towards a stream. The sound of tumbling water drifts over from the right. At the stream turn right for a few steps to a little bridge where the path crosses it. There is then a magnificent view of the waterfall that previously could only be heard. It is a beautiful cascade that tumbles and splashes over huge boulders piled high above you. In fact, here you stand below the dam that for more than 200 years has held back the waters of Virginia Stream to form Virginia Water.

Climb up the bank to the left of the waterfall and continue along the path with the lake again to your right. Two hundred yards bring you to a broad grassy area with two rows of ancient stone columns in a railed enclosure over to the left, (see notes). Unseen beyond the road behind the ruins is Fort Belvedere where Edward VIII signed the Document of Abdication in 1936.

The path continues with the bushes and lofty old hardwood trees of Frostfarm Plantation to the left and with the tranquil waters of the lake to the right. Later, a group of estate workers' cottages comes into view on the opposite shore and then a path goes off left for 150 yards to Blacknest car park. Half-right ahead an impressive five-arched grey stone bridge, named High Bridge, has come into view across the water. Continue forward along the main path. Past Blacknest car park it swings around to the right, crosses a little bridge and then, as you approach a pink walled gate lodge, swings right to join a metalled road that runs through the park. (If you go out of the park by this gate and turn left you can obtain refreshments at the Seven Stars public house on the A.329 road only 150 yards along it.)

Proceed along this road and head towards High Bridge 300 yards away. The bridge spans an upper arm of the lake that winds placidly away to the left between thickly wooded banks. Once over the bridge the road cuts across a broad open greensward that is a popular place for picnics. To the right is the isolated group of houses that was first seen from the other side of the lake, near

WALK TWO

Blacknest. The road eventually curves down to a white-railed causeway to cross another side-arm of the lake. The sheet of water backed up for 450 yards to the left is called Johnson's Pond.

Just beyond the causeway the path divides into three. The middle path, signed towards the Heather Garden and Valley Garden is the most attractive and therefore the one to follow. It goes up the forward slope and over the shoulder of High Flyer's Hill where it is quickly engulfed by a shrub garden. The path meanders among endless varieties of azaleas, magnolias, rhododendrons and other exotic flowering shrubs. In April and May its array of blossoms is a sheer delight. In October it puts on another blaze of colour when the leaves take on their various autumn hues. There are several smaller gardens within the extensive Valley Garden. (see notes).

When it is time to leave these exquisite gardens, make your way downhill to rejoin the lakeside path. Follow it to Botany Bay Point, opposite the Leptis Magna ruins on the far shore, where it angles away from the waterside once more. Take care to avoid a turning on the left running parallel with the route of the walk; ignore the path and keep on the main track. The walk then goes over a slight rise and through old established woodland for about 500 yards. It then descends again towards the water. Unexpectedly, in a grassy clearing, you will arrive in front of a towering 100 feet high pole with weird carved and painted figures running its whole length. It is an authentic Red Indian totem pole carved by Canadian Indians about 25 years ago (see notes).

Go down towards the water from the totem pole. The path crosses an attractive creek by a causeway. A small waterfall feeds the spillage from Wick Pond on the left to the main lake on the right. An easy walk of ¾ mile will then take you back along the lakeside to the car park where the walk commenced.

Virginia Water - Historical Notes

Virginia Water: An artificial lake created about 1750 by Thomas Sandby for the Duke of Cumberland. The Duke was the brother of George III. He had conclusively beaten the Scots under Bonnie Prince Charlie at Culloden and had been rewarded with the Rangership of Windsor Great Park. Much of the present appearance of the park results from the landscaping work done under his direction. Virginia Water was enlarged to its present area of about

200 acres late in the eighteenth century. George IV had a scaled down frigate built for the lake. It was still in use in Queen Victoria's reign and was brought out at her request. A lieutenant and six sailors sailed it along the lake and fired a royal salute from its cannon.

It is perhaps ironic that the victor of Culloden (who was afterwards known as 'Butcher' Cumberland) should have created such beautiful landscape so close to the possible site of even greater butchery in AD60 - that of the final battle between the Roman 14th Legion and Queen Boudicca's army of Britons in rebellion. There are sound reasons (see *London Archaeologist* Autumn 1983 issue) for believing the site to have been between Callow Hill and Knowl Hill - certainly it fulfils Tacitus' description of the Roman position being approached by a narrow defile with a wood behind and a plain in front.

Leptis Magna Ruins: These are the genuine remains of a fine Roman building recovered from Leptis Magna near Tripoli in North Africa. They were brought to England and presented to the Prince Regent in 1816. A proposal to use them for the portico of the British Museum never materialised and they were set up here as a landscape ornament in 1826.

Valley Garden: A beautiful twentieth century shrub garden covering some 300 acres. It is designed never to be without interesting flowers or foliage. It was begun in 1935 with the planting of Pinetum Valley. Other sections have followed since. West of Pinetum Valley is a hydrangea garden established in 1963. East of the Pinetum is the Heather Garden that has been developed since 1954 in a former gravel pit. Further to the east are camelias and the Punch Bowl filled with evergreen azaleas.

Totem Pole: This 100 feet high totem pole is carved from a single log of western red cedar *(thuja plicata)* which is native to British Columbia and the neighbouring region. The tree from which it came was 600 years old when felled. The totem pole is carved and painted throughout its length in the traditional style of North American Indians. It was carved to commemorate the centenary of British Columbia in 1958. It was presented to the Queen during her visit there and subsequently shipped to England and erected here.

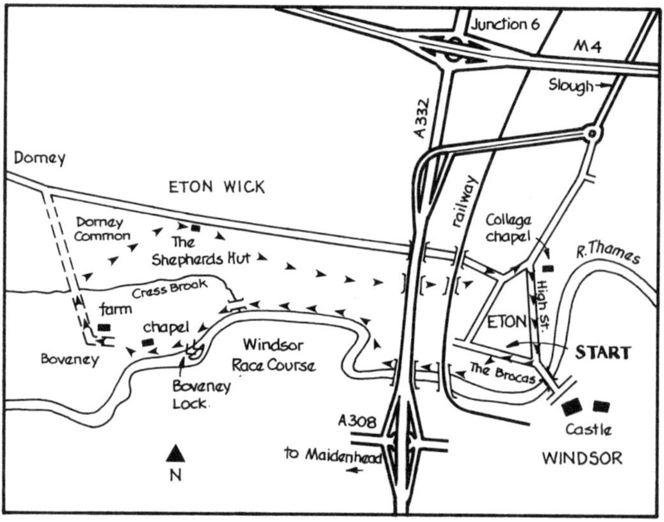
Junction 6
M4
Slough
A332
Dorney
ETON WICK
railway
Dorney Common
The Shepherds Hut
College chapel
R. Thames
Cress Brook
farm
chapel
ETON
High St.
Boveney
Windsor Race Course
START
The Brocas
Boveney Lock
A308
Castle
to Maidenhead
WINDSOR
N

WALK THREE

Eton: with Boveney and Dorney Common

Introduction: The setting for this walk is the small but precious area of countryside that lies between Maidenhead, Slough and Windsor. Despite being so close to these modern towns it is pleasantly rural. The route is based on Eton, a small attractive townlet across the river from Windsor. The town is dominated by the famous public school that carries its name. Eton College buildings date back, in some instances, for as much as 500 years and some of them can be visited. Bearing this in mind, why not spend a whole day at Eton? Use the morning, say, to follow the walk through the surrounding countryside and the afternoon to explore the College and the town.

The walk leaves Eton and crosses a meadow called The Brocas to the Thames, where it follows the river upstream to Boveney Lock and on to an old chapel, strangely alone among waterside meadows. The walk then goes through the pretty hamlet of Boveney to Dorney Common, beautifully broad and green and typical of the commons that were once an essential feature of English villages. The route goes quickly through Eton Wick where there is an opportunity to obtain refreshments. It returns to Eton across level meadows on what was once the great South Field of the local manor. It goes under the modern A.355 road and Brunel's Windsor Branch Railway to re-enter Eton among college buildings. It arrives at the main street opposite the west front of the magnificent fifteenth century College Chapel. The route then travels the length of High Street which is crammed with antique shops and restaurants, and then returns to The Brocas where it began. The route is completely level. The paths are all easily found and provide good walking.

WALK THREE

Distance: This walk is 5½ miles long and will take about 2¼ hours to complete.

Refreshments: There are many restaurants, cafes and pubs in Eton where refreshments can be had at the beginning and end of the walk. Additionally, at The Shepherd's Hut in Eton Wick, sandwiches and light snacks are always on offer. A few doors along from The Shepherds Hut there is a fish and chip shop. They are passed approximately ⅔ of the way around the route.

How to get there: Eton is easily reached on foot from Windsor which is well served by buses and trains. If driving, enter Eton and follow the High Street towards Windsor. Just before the river bridge (now closed to traffic) turn right into Brocas Street. After 250 yards turn left into Meadow Lane. Park beside this lane in an area provided on the left-hand side about 200 yards ahead. This is where the walk starts. If coming on foot from Windsor take the first turning to the left after crossing the river bridge. This is Brocas Street and leads to the starting place described above.

The walk: Leave the parking place in Meadow Lane and go through a gap in the hedge to the meadow called The Brocas (see notes). Angle right and go over to the river's edge. Windsor is on the opposite bank and the whole area is overlooked by its great grey stone castle.

Turn right and follow the river upstream. Go under an iron railway bridge and a concrete road bridge. 100 yards past the concrete bridge turn right onto a footpath that goes away from the river. It comes back to the water's edge about 250 yards further on after having cut off a huge 'U' bend in the river. The route goes on beside the Thames. The houses of Eton Wick can be seen across the meadows to the right and Windsor Racecourse shows between the trees on the left bank of the river. The path crosses a wooden footbridge over a sidestream and, ½ mile further on, crosses swift-flowing Boveney Ditch just where it flows into the Thames. Another 600 yards beside the river brings the path to Boveney Lock set among well-kept lawns and flower gardens.

A track to Boveney angles to the right and follows a line of horse chestnut trees between open meadows. It is more interesting and only a little further if you keep on beside the river for another ¼ mile. The path then comes to a stone-and-flint chapel standing alone near the river (see notes).

Leave the chapel of St Mary Magdalene and follow the lane directly away from the river. 200 yards along is an open area and a little tarmac road. Turn left and follow this road between the attractive old houses of Boveney. It turns sharply to the right by Boveney Court Farm and then goes out onto a broad open grassy area. This is Dorney Common. 300 yards past the farm the road crosses Cress Brook. Leave the road here and strike off to the right across the common. Keep the brook on your right-hand side and head for the red and brown roofs of Eton Wick ½ mile away across the level grazing land.

The route meets a quiet motor road at the edge of Eton Wick. Go over a cattle grid and into the village. Follow the main street for nearly ½ a mile. It passes shops and The Shepherd's Hut public house where refreshments can be had during "hours".

When the main street reaches the village hall turn right between the hall and a modern church. Go for 150 yards along Hayward's Mead with a recreation ground on the right-hand side. At the end of Hayward's Mead continue in the same direction along a bridle path. It soon leaves the last houses of Eton Wick behind and goes between unfenced crop fields. Windsor Castle is skylined directly ahead. Ignore crossing paths and head towards a row of five flood tunnels beneath the elevated road that links Slough with Windsor. Across the field to the right is the River Thames and the path that was used in the outward route.

The route then goes under the elevated road by way of the flood tunnels. It continues for 200 yards along a field edge to the Windsor branch railway line (see notes) supported on an endless series of brown brick arches that carry it over the flood plain. Go under the railway, and you will find the path then angles left for 150 yards to meet a tarmac road by the first buildings of Eton. Turn right and meander with this road for ¼ mile into the town. It meets the main street at a 'T' junction with traffic lights. Directly opposite is the famous Eton College Chapel (see notes). This is a good point to break off from the route if you intend to tour the college buildings (see notes).

The walking route turns right at the traffic lights and goes the length of High Street, which is very attractive, crammed with antique shops and restaurants. It goes by The Cockpit, a beautiful old timbered building with the parish stocks and whipping post outside. At the end of High Street, a few yards before it meets the river bridge, turn right into Brocas Street. Then it winds for 250

WALK THREE

yards and goes by Eton College Boathouses. Turn left by a pay-and-display car park and follow Meadow Lane for 200 yards back to the starting place by The Brocas.

Eton - Historical Notes

The Brocas: A pleasant meadow beside the Thames. It has been owned since 1504 by Eton College and is open to the public. The name commemorates the Brocas family of Clewer who were prominent in this area during the Middle Ages. One of them, Sir John, had bought the land in 1321. Another of them, Sir Bernard, was a friend of The Black Prince. He is connected, in legend at least, with the events that led to the founding of the Order of the Garter by Edward III in 1348. Sir Bernard's son supported Richard II and took part in a desperate attempt to free him from the Tower of London. This escapade cost him his head and earned a mention in Shakespeare's play, "Richard II".

Boveney Church: The Chapel of St. Mary Magdalene is an attractive building of flint and rubblestone with a weatherboarded bellcot. Parts of the building date back to the thirteenth century and the site is even older. Its origins are obscure. There is a belief that it was built here beside the river to provide a place of worship for bargees and rivermen. It is also said to have been a chapel of ease for neighbouring Boveney Court which was once owned by Burnham Abbey. There is evidence now to suggest that houses of the village once clustered much closer to the river and that the church was then among them and not strangely distanced from them as now. The key to the church can be obtained from Old Place, the house to the north of it.

Windsor Branch Railway: Despite vigorous opposition from the Provost of Eton College, an act of Parliament in 1848 authorised the branch line to Windsor. Work began immediately and the line was opened the following year. It was carried over the flood plain on wooden trestles. These were replaced by the present brick arches in 1861-5.

Eton College: This is the second-oldest school in Britain. It was founded in 1440 by King Henry VI. His idea was to transfer scholars from Eton to King's College, Cambridge (founded in the following year) when they were sufficiently educated. The school was intended to form part of an even larger foundation which was to include a community of secular priests, a pilgrimage church and an almshouse. Many of Henry's plans had to be modified after he was deposed in 1461. The oldest part of the school dates from 1443 and there are in use buildings from each of the four following centuries also. A very pleasant circuit of the school precincts can be made by entering School Yard and going under Lupton's Tower to The Cloisters. Go through towards College Field and circle back through Weston's Yard to the main road. Visitors are admitted to the school's historic buildings during the afternoon in term time in summer and from 10.30am during the school holidays. Entrance fee is 60p; children and pensioners 20p. From April to October there are two daily guided tours: at 2.15pm and 3.30pm. These last approximately an hour. Fees for the guided tours are 80p and 50p respectively. Parties intending to take a guided tour must book in advance by letter. Write to the Tourist Manager, Eton College, Eton, Windsor, Berkshire.

Eton College Chapel: If Henry VI's plans had been fulfilled the present chapel would be merely the choir of a much grander church. Nonetheless it is a most beautiful and impressive building. It is in the perpendicular style with lofty columns rising to a superb vaulted ceiling which is a modern completion of the original design. The chapel walls have on them what are probably the finest fifteenth century wall paintings in the country. They were painted between 1479 and 1487. A Protestant edict resulted in them being whitewashed over in 1560 and they remained undiscovered until 1847. They were not finally fully revealed until 1923 when Victorian stall canopies were taken out. Subsequent cleaning and restoration which was completed in 1975 now shows them in their true glory.

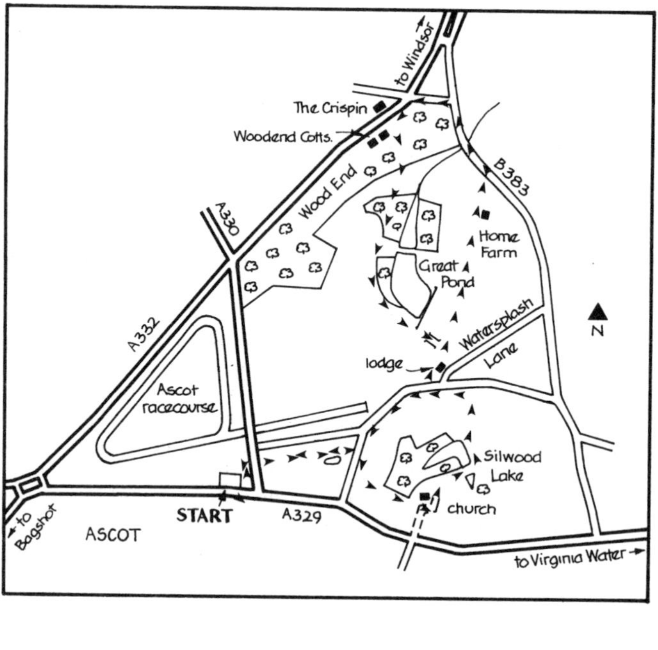
to Windsor
The Crispin
Woodend Cotts.
Wood End
B383
A330
Home Farm
Great Pond
Watersplash Lane
N
A332
lodge
Ascot racecourse
Silwood Lake
church
to Bagshot
START
A329
ASCOT
to Virginia Water

WALK FOUR

Ascot - Through Windsor Forest and The Crown Estate

Introduction: This walk is in traditional oak-studded Windsor Forest countryside and part of it goes through the Crown Estate. It is quite close to Ascot, Sunningdale and Windsor yet is very pleasantly rural. The paths are well defined and easy to follow and there are no steep hills to climb. The way goes through oakwoods, pine plantations and gently rolling meadowland. It offers a good chance of seeing many varieties of woodland birds as you go through.

Distance: The route is 6 miles long and takes about 2¾ hours to walk.

Refreshments: There are a number of inns in Ascot, near the start and finish of the walk. The Crispin public house is passed approximately half way round the circuit and offers morning coffee and cold buffet in addition to the usual refreshments.

How to get there: The walk begins at one of the official car parks attached to the renowned racecourse at Ascot. It is the "No. 6 Silver Ring Car Park" and is found beside the A.329 main road at the Virginia Water end of Ascot's main street. It is used as a free public car park except during the June and July race meetings. Headroom at the entrance is restricted to 6'9".

The walk: Leave the car park and turn left along London Road. Walk away from the shopping centre for 100 yards and then turn left into Winkfield Road and follow it for 300 yards. Royal Ascot Racecourse crosses the road here, and there is a good view of the main buildings and the modern grandstand over to the left. (see notes).

WALK FOUR

Retrace your steps for a few yards along Winkfield Road and turn left onto a footpath. The path goes alongside a broad area of turf that is part of Ascot Heath. It is straight for the ½ mile to Cheapside Road which it meets beside an imposing pair of wrought-iron gates with gilded upper parts and supported by stone pillars with statues and shields on top.

Turn right and walk for 300 yards along Cheapside Road. Pass some modern houses on the right and two entrances to Tetworth Hall on the left. A footpath then goes off to the left between meadows. Turn onto it and follow it downhill. One field-width to the right is the traffic on the Ascot to Virginia Water road and on the rise to the left is bow-fronted Tetworth Hall. The path goes into a wood, passes a cottage on the right and then comes to a little rust-coloured stream. After crossing the stream by a footbridge follow the path through the trees on the other side. Soon the wood gives way to scattered oak trees with bracken covering the ground between them.

The path continues its gentle climb, and at the top of the rise it goes forward onto a made-up road in front of St. Michael's Church, Sunninghill (see notes). Go straight over the road and on to a surfaced path that runs alongside the churchyard. After 75 yards the path swings to the left and goes behind the church. Follow it for nearly 200 yards to an iron kissing gate which gives way to a footpath.

The footpath angles to the right and descends, between fields, towards a wood. The countryside here is attractive rolling meadowland that is fairly heavily wooded. At the bottom of the slope the path goes through a gate and into the wood. Almost immediately it crosses an upper arm of Silwood Lake and swings around to the left. It then follows the lakeside for about 200 yards before swinging to the right, away from the water. Another 50 yards bring it to a tall iron kissing gate on the right-hand side. Five paces beyond it there is a narrow footpath going off to the left between wire fences. Turn left onto this footpath. In a short while it crosses a stream and passes a beautiful black and white timber framed house before climbing gently to meet a motor road among houses at Cheapside.

Turn left and walk for 100 yards along the road to the junction where Watersplash Lane goes off to the right. Next to this turning is East Lodge and a private drive that leads into the Crown Estate. Turn right into this drive. There is a pedestrian right-of-way along it. Go by the lodge with its pink-washed walls and thatched roof. Continue downhill between plantations of conifer trees. 150 yards from the public road there is a stile on the left-hand side where the return route rejoins the outward route.

Continue walking straight ahead. The drive has a good surface for much of the way. The countryside is dotted with old Windsor Forest oaks and is very attractive. Where the track begins to climb, it is badly rutted by tractors. As it nears Home Farm at the top of its rise it becomes difficult to pass dry-footed. The right-of-way goes straight ahead, through gates and between the farm buildings, and 100 yards past the farmyard the track comes to a motor road.

Turn left onto this road. It is the B.383 Sunninghill to Windsor road. Climb gently with it for ½ mile until, exactly at the top of its rise, The B.3034 goes off to the left. It is signposted to Winkfield and Maidenhead. Go along it for 200 yards to a cross-roads in front of The Crispin public house.

Turn left at the cross-roads and walk for 150 yards along the A.332 in the direction of Ascot. The Crispin is now on your right-hand side. When about 40 yards past it, turn left onto a footpath. It will take you past the entrance drive to Woodend Cottages and, as a sign-board advises, enters the Crown Estate once more. The path then goes beside Woodend Cottages and between plantations of lofty old conifer trees with an attractive carpet of bracken beneath. The footpath continues through Wood End, as this corner of the estate is known. It then goes down a short slope to a stile and crosses a wide grassy forest ride. It goes over another stile and crosses a meadow before plunging on again between plantations.

Continue along the path. Woods and meadows alternate alongside. After half a mile a big open sheet of water called Great Pond, is just visible through the trees to the left. The path continues to a 'T' junction where a drive crosses from left to right. If you take a few steps to the left there is a lovely uninterrupted view up Great Pond from the earth dam that holds back its waters. The forward route goes straight on from the junction where the path met the drive. A footpath goes downhill through trees and bushes; its line confirmed by signposts. The way crosses a stream by a railed footbridge. Continue along the path for another two or three minutes. It then climbs to a stile that allows it out of the wood onto the made-up drive that was walked earlier. Turn right,

WALK FOUR

and it is only 150 yards to the pink-walled East Lodge and Cheapside road.

There is a choice of return routes from here. You can either turn left and follow the outward paths back to Ascot or turn right and take a shorter route. If you turn right, follow the road for a little over ¼ mile to a junction where a side road goes off to the right. Continue along the main road for another 250 yards to the big iron gates at the entrance to Ascot Heath. Immediately past them a familiar footpath goes off to the right. Go back along this footpath for the ½ mile to Winkfield Road. Turn left along Winkfield Road to its 'T' junction with the A.327. Turn right towards Ascot centre and the car park where the walk began will be found 100 yards along on the right-hand side.

Ascot - Historical Notes

Ascot Racecouse: This is situated on Ascot Heath. Horseracing was started here in 1711 by Queen Anne. The meetings only really became popular when they were revived by The Duke of Cumberland later in the eighteenth century. He was Ranger of Windsor Great Park and kept his stud there at what is now Cumberland Lodge. The long, curving grandstand at Ascot was built in the 1960's and is an impressive modern structure. The Queen frequently drives from Windsor, through The Great Park, to attend race meetings here.

St. Michael's Church, Sunninghill: The church was entirely rebuilt in the early nineteenth century. The chancel, chapel and vestry were added in 1888. The building is of brown brick with crenelated tower and walls. The west door is framed by an arch of original twelfth century carved Norman stonework. The arch was discovered in the kitchen block of a local house and was restored to the church in 1926.

WALK FIVE

The Haunt of Highwaymen: Maidenhead Thicket

Introduction: This walk begins in Maidenhead Thicket, a renowned beauty spot owned by the National Trust. It visits an Iron Age enclosure before leaving the trees and going over open farmland to Burchett's Green. It goes on to Ashley Hill where it climbs through beautiful Forestry Commission plantations to the summit. The route then makes a right turn and descends through the trees to the pretty and remote Dew Drop Inn. It goes on over open farmland to Hall Place, once the grand home of local landowners and now the central building of Berkshire College of Agriculture. The path then angles across to Burchett's Green and rejoins the outward route. The last mile of the walk returns along the path used on the outward journey.

The route is a little over 5 miles long and will take about 2½ hours to walk.

Refreshments: There are two pubs on the route; The Crown in Burchett's Green and The Dew Drop just north of Ashley Hill. The first is passed both on the outward and the return sections of the walk and the second is placed about half-way round the circuit. The Crown always has rolls and pies available. The Dew Drop offers snacks and hot meals in the bar from Monday to Saturday lunchtimes and Tuesday to Saturday evenings.

How to get there: Maidenhead Thicket is beside the A.4 road on the west side of Maidenhead barely two miles from the town centre. Make your way to the roundabout where the A.4 crosses the A423 road towards Henley: the same roundabout where a spur of the M.4 motorway ends. Head along the A.423 towards Henley for 400 yards and then turn left onto a track that plunges

WALK FIVE

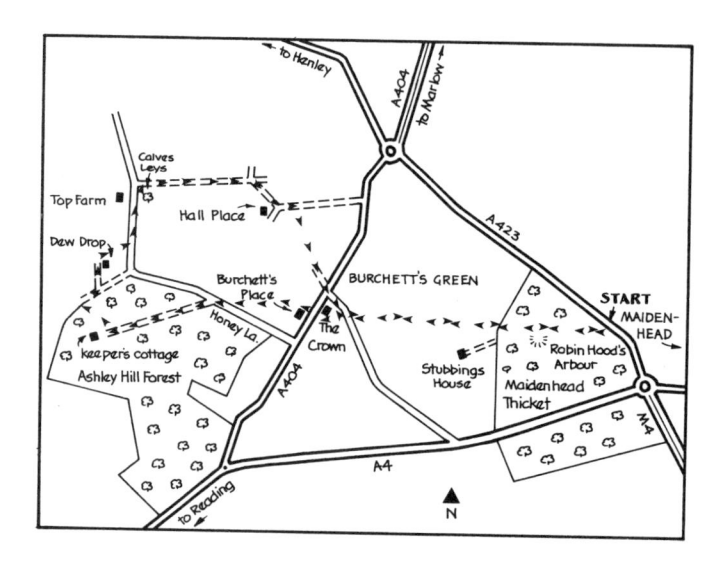

into the Thicket. Cars may be parked beside this track and this is the place from which to start.

The walk: The greater part of Maidenhead Thicket lies within the angle formed by the A.4 and the A.423. It is owned by the National Trust and is freely open to the public at all times. There has been a thicket here for centuries. Now it is a beautiful tract of tranquil woodland but once it was a much feared haunt of highwaymen who preyed on coaches travelling the Great West Road; the present-day A.4.

Walk away from the road. The straight and level track is lined with majestic old limes, horse chestnuts and oaks that rise high above the dense tangle of smaller trees and bushes that form the thicket. In spring the ground is carpeted with wood violets and bluebells and in autumn the bushes are all entwined with the wispy grey tufts of old man's beard.

600 yards from the road the track goes by Robin Hood's Arbour on the left. This romantic name has been given to an enclosure surrounded by a ditch that was constructed by the Ancient Britons

2000 years ago. An information board there draws attention to it and explains its interesting history. (see notes).

Continue along the main track. A number of paths and rides go off to each side and lead to tree-ringed glades that make beautiful picnic places. It is 400 yards from Robin Hood's Arbour to a junction of paths at the edge of the wood. Half-left is the entrance drive to Stubbings House (see notes). Maintain the same forward direction. Go onto a footpath that follows along the right-hand edge of the gate lodge's garden and after negotiating a stile continue onwards with a copse to the left and a spaced line of horse chestnuts to the right. The path is easily followed. The route then proceeds over more stiles and follows field edges across a level farming landscape. Ahead are the houses of Burchett's Green with the low dome of Ashley Hill rising directly behind them. One mile from the start, go through the barnyard of Stubbings Farm and emerge onto a quiet motor road.

Turn right along this road and follow along it for 100 yards to a 'T' junction by The Crown, a red brick inn on the left. Turn left onto the A.404 road and walk in the direction signed towards Reading. After 200 yards turn right onto a footpath that leaves the road between an attractive pair of cottages and a large modern house called Burchett's Place.

This footpath is well used and easily followed although sometimes muddy. It maintains the general direction of the walk so far and follows field margins over pleasant level countryside. Away to the right is imposing Hall Place, a large country house now used by Berkshire College of Agriculture. (The return route goes through its grounds.) After 600 yards this path leads to a little spinney where it spills out onto a quiet by-lane called Honey Lane.

Turn right and climb gently for 250 yards along this lane. Then, at the point where it swings sharply to the right, take to a tarmac drive that goes off to the left. A five-bar gate prevents the entry of vehicles but not walkers. A notice board advises that this is Forestry Commission land and that the wood is called Ashley Hill Wood. Follow the drive uphill into the wood. There are plantations of several different kinds of trees alongside. Perhaps you can identify the various species as you walk through. The drive is enclosed by the trees and is a beautifully secluded section of the walk. Some areas of the woods are carpeted with bluebells in May whilst other have a thick undergrowth of bracken later in the year.

WALK FIVE

It takes only a short time to reach the top of the hill where the tarmac drive enters a clearing and leads to a secluded house called Keeper's Cottage. This is the highest point reached during the walk and is a lovely spot to pause for a rest or a picnic.

Continue the walk by turning right just outside the grounds of Keeper's Cottage. Follow an attractive grassy track that cuts downhill through the woods. The trees to the left are larch and those to the right are beech. Both are especially beautiful in May and again in October when they wear their spring and autumn colours. There is a long forward view as you go down. It reaches across to the Thames at Medmenham and to the hills beyond. The track narrows at the bottom of its descent and then spills out onto a hard track that crosses it from left to right.

Turn right along this track. It has the appearance of a medieval lane and could be miles away from civilisation. It runs for 250 yards along the bottom edge of Ashley Hill Wood and then goes through a gate to join a narrow made-up-road. Turn left along the made-up road. In less than 50 yards it arrives quite unexpectedly at a pub. The Dew Drop Inn is a pretty flint-and-brick building with lots of rustic garden furniture outside. It is probably the most secluded pub in the country.

The little road ends at the Dew Drop. Maintain the same forward direction by going onto a narrow footpath that meanders for 100 yards between bushes and brambles. It then emerges into the open by a five-bar gate. Go through the gate and, within a dozen paces, turn right and follow along the right-hand side of a fence that divides two meadows. There are distant views to the left but those to the right are cut short by the swell of Ashley Hill rising from the other side of this meadow. Half-left is a large group of buildings that belong to Top Farm. At the end of this field the path goes out onto a quiet motor road which is another section of Honey Lane; the lane from which the walk entered Ashley Hill Wood.

Turn left along Honey Lane and go by the barn-yard entrance to Top Farm. Immediately past the farm buildings turn right. Go onto a little concrete road than runs straight and level. There is a wood on its right-hand side called Calves Leys and open farmland to the left. 100 yards past the wood there are stiles at each side of the road where a footpath crosses.

Continue along the concrete road until it goes among the outbuildings of Berkshire Agricultural College at Hall Place. At a cross-ways, where the forward track is unsurfaced, turn right. Follow the road round for 130 yards until it meets the main entrance drive to Hall Place. Just across to the right is the impressive red brick house towering over the attendant buildings that have clustered around it since it was taken over by the Agricultural College. (see notes).

Turn left and head down the main entrance drive into Hall Place. It is a straight road between two impressive rows of old lime trees with dark clumps of mistletoe in their upper branches.

Leave the main drive after 100 yards. Turn right and follow a well-trodden footpath that goes for 400 yards across an open field. Head towards a red brick house at the far side of the field where the path goes through a tall iron kissing gate. A straight grassy path then goes for 50 yards between hedges to a little lane with a made-up surface. The lane goes away to the right. Follow it between attractive houses and cottages for 300 yards to the A.404 road which it meets opposite The Crown in Burchett's Green.

Go straight across the main road and into the lane beside the pub. Follow it for just 50 yards to the point where it turns sharply to the right by Burchett's Green Farm. Leave the road and go onto a footpath that goes off to the left at the bend. This is the same footpath that was used on the outward route. It goes by the barns of Burchett's Green Farm and along the edges of fields to the gate lodge at the entrance to Stubbings House. Go across the drive and follow the forward track into Maidenhead Thicket. It goes by Robin Hood's Arbour and back to the starting place.

Maidenhead Thicket - Historical Notes

Maidenhead Thicket: 368 acres of dense woodland owned by the National Trust. There has been a thicket here for centuries. During the Stage Coach Era it was notorious as a haunt of highwaymen. Such celebrated "gentlemen of the road" as Claud Duval and John Clark (sentenced to death in 1740) preyed upon travellers on the Great West Road and on those travelling towards Henley and Oxford. It is said that in the late 1500's the vicars of Hurley were paid considerable danger money for the risks they took in going through the thicket on their weekly journeys to Maidenhead.

WALK FIVE

Robin Hood's Arbour: It has no connection with the legendary Robin. It is a late Iron Age enclosure approximately 60 paces square. The surrounding ditch is less than knee-deep and 6 to 8 feet wide, but excavations have shown that originally it was 2'9" deep and 16 feet wide. The gap in the west side is an original entrance. Pottery fragments found here have been dated to the first half of the first century AD. This suggests that the enclosure was built by the Ancient Britons shortly before the Roman Conquest. A National Trust information board at the site gives a full description of its history.

Stubbings House: This was the home-in-exile of Queen Wilhelmina of the Netherlands whilst her country was occupied by the Germans during the Second World War. Her military bodyguard was encamped at Robin Hood's Arbour.

Burchett's Green: Commonly spelled Birchets or Birches Green on old maps. A barn at Stubbings Farm is estimated to be about 400 years old. Seventeenth century Woodlands Cottage was once a Friends' Meeting House.

Ashley Hill: The hill rises to 475 feet above sea level and 375 feet above the Thames. It was a favourite lookout point for highwaymen waiting for likely victims to come along the Bath Road. Ashely Hill has been written as Alleyhill Coppes on old maps. Deer in the woods are probably descended from the herd that once roamed Hall Place park.

Dew Drop Inn: The Inn is said to have been founded for the benefit of Windsor Forest workers.

Hall Place: It was among the possessions of Hurley Priory at its dissolution. In 1728 it was bought by William East whose descendants held it until the 1940s when Berkshire County Council took it over. It is now an Agricultural Training College. The present house was built soon after 1728 on the site of its larger predecessor. It is of red brick in the style of the French Renaissance. Druids are said to haunt the house and a ghostly horse and carriage are said to cross the back lawn. The ghost of a black servant has been reported at Black Horse Bridge. One of the former occupants, Sir Robert Clayton, was Lord Mayor of London in 1688. He received the Prince of Orange into The City where later he was crowned King William III in place of James II who had fled.

WALK SIX

Cookham and Bourne End

Introduction: This walk is centred on the pretty and popular Thames-side village of Cookham. The route begins at Cookham Moor and goes through the centre of the village. It visits the Stanley Spencer Gallery where original paintings by this renowned Cookham artist are on show. The route goes by the church to the riverside and then along the towing-path to Cock Marsh, a large National Trust area below the slopes of Winter Hill. It veers away from the river and circles back to Cookham Moor by different paths. The paths are all good and easily followed. Cookham and its surroundings are understandably very popular with visitors and walkers as the village and the route are extremely attractive and provide a very pleasant outing.

Distance: 3¾ miles which will take about 1¾ hours to walk.

Refreshments: There are several pubs and cafes in Cookham. During summer week-ends an ice cream van visits the riverside near the sailing club. The route goes by the Moorings Hotel and Cap'n Hook's Bar where snacks or hot meals can be had "during hours" every day during the summer and on Saturdays and Sundays from November to March. It is approximately ⅓ of the way around the circuit.

How to get there: Cookham can be approached from Marlow, Bourne End or Maidenhead. A minor road from Marlow goes through Cookham Dean and Cookham Rise before crossing Cookham Moor. Stop here and leave the car in the National Trust car park. If coming from Bourne End, cross the Thames by Cookham Bridge and take the second turning to the right, which is High Street. If coming from Maidenhead on the A.4094 turn left

WALK SIX

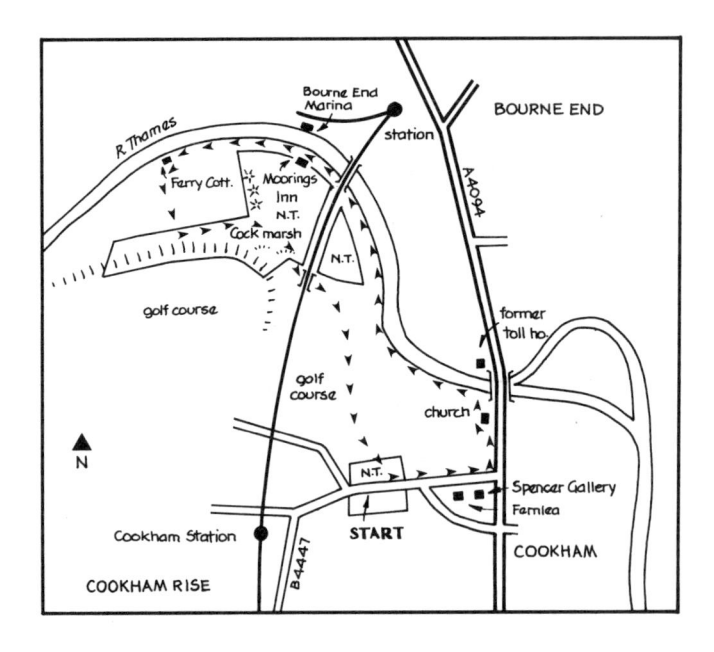

into High Street and go straight through to the car park at Cookham Moor. If coming by train, Cookham Moor is just ⅓ mile down the slope from Cookham Station.

The walk: Start from the car parking area at Cookham Moor. Angle across the grass to the road and turn left towards the village. Pass the War Memorial and enter High Street. Go by the Old Forge (nearly five centuries old) and continue past the attractive buildings from most periods on each side of the road. There is a circular blue plaque on one Victorian house which states that it is the birthplace of Sir Stanley Spencer (see notes). At the end of High Street, on the right-hand corner, is a former chapel that now houses the Spencer Gallery (see notes).

Turn left at the end of High Street. Across the main road Ferry Lane goes off to the right. Beside a stone seat at the junction is The Tarrystone, a large old sarsen with a metal plaque fixed to the

34

front of it (see notes). The main road veers right towards Cookham Bridge. Ignore it and follow the left curve between attractive white-walled houses to Holy Trinity Church (see notes). Go through the churchyard to the riverside. The church grounds are filled with daffodils and blossom in spring and with roses during summer.

At the river's edge, if you look to the right you will have a good view of Cookham Bridge (see notes). Turn left and walk alongside the river. For 200 yards the way goes through an area of mown grass and park benches. It then goes past a sailing club and out into open countryside. The river is now edged with willows and there are crop fields to the left. Continue alongside the river and go under the latticed iron bridge that carries the Bourne End branch railway line. You next pass in front of some waterside bungalows and the Moorings Inn with Cap'n Hook's Bar. Across the river is Bourne End Marina packed with white-hulled cruisers.

The path leaves the houses behind and goes into a broad grassy area called Cock Marsh (see notes). The route follows the river along Spade Oak Reach to Ferry Cottage where Spade Oak Ferry used to operate. See the ferryman's clapboard kiosk still in the garden. The path leaves the riverside here and goes for 300 yards behind an isolated row of houses that front onto the river. It then turns left in the corner of a field and heads directly away from the river. It goes over open, level cropfields, crosses a stile and goes on towards a steep grassy hillside which has a track angling upwards across it towards Winter Hill away to the right.

At the base of the hillside the path meets a level grassy track that runs along under it. Turn left onto this track. It goes above the soft areas of Cock Marsh and provides good firm walking. There are frequently large numbers of lapwings (also called peewits or green plovers) wheeling over the Marsh and beyond are distant views of the Chiltern Hills.

An arch of dark brown bricks takes the path under the Bourne End branch railway to the corner of Winter Hill Golf Course. Enter the golf course and go along its left-hand edge, close to a wire fence. Follow alongside this fence for 200 yards to a stile with "footpath" signs on a post beside it. Cross the fence here and turn right to resume the same direction but now just outside the golf course. The route has returned to within about 40 yards of the Thames and there are attractive views of Cookham, its church and slim iron river bridge.

WALK SIX

The path here is clearly defined. It goes along a level bank with tall hedges to the right and a drainage ditch following all the way along the left-hand edge. In a ¼ mile the path comes to a gate with a stile beside it. Cross the stile and go into the small meadow in front. Go along its left-hand side, still following the drainage ditch. At the far corner of this meadow go over another stile, cross a little concrete footbridge and go through a hedge to emerge back at Cookham Moor car park.

Cookham - Historical Notes

Fernley: A Victorian semi-detached house in High Street where Stanley Spencer, Cookham's most famous inhabitant, was born in 1891. The pair of houses were built by Spencer's grandfather. After the Second World War Stanley Spencer returned to Fernley which had been bought for him by Lord Astor and Jack Martineau.

Sir Stanley Spencer Gallery: This is in King's Hall, a former Wesleyan Chapel, and was opened in 1962. It is unique in that it is devoted solely to the life and work of one artist and is in the village of his birth. The exhibition consists of sketches, paintings and personal mementoes of the artist. Spencer based many of his paintings on locally recognisable scenes. Those in the exhibition are changed twice a year and are augmented by loans from private and public collections. The winter exhibition, November to Easter, is open Saturdays, Sundays and bank holidays 11am to 1pm and 2pm to 5pm. The summer exhibition is open daily 10.30am to 1pm and 2pm to 6pm except Saturdays, Sundays and bank holidays when it closes at 6.30pm.

Tarrystone: A large sarsen stone historically used as a boundary marker and variously said to have been sited at different ends of High Street. It spent most of the nineteenth century as an ornament in a private garden but was recovered for the village and placed in its present position in 1905. In Tudor times the village held a sports day "at the Cookham Stone" (Tarrystone) on Assumption Day.

Holy Trinity Church, Cookham: Parts of the building can be dated to the 12th century. The nave is early Norman and the chancel is almost as old. There are medieval tiles in the chancel and the tower was built about 1500. There is a considerable amount of clunch (chalk block) in the building. It may well have come from Bisham Wood where an ancient chalk mine is known to have existed. Chalk pits in Cookham produced only soft chalk which was unsuitable for building.

Cookham Bridge: The present iron structure is the second bridge to span the Thames just here. It was built in 1867 and replaced a short-lived wooden bridge. It has been described as "the cheapest bridge across the Thames" and was a toll bridge until 1947. The toll house, a little octagonal brick building, still stands beside it on the far bank.

Cock Marsh: A large open area of grass beside the Thames. It covers 132 acres and is owned by the National Trust. There are four prehistoric burial mounds (bowl barrows) plainly visible above the level ground. The largest is 90 feet in diameter and 7 feet high. Three were excavated during the nineteenth century. Two of them contained early Bronze Age burials from almost 4,000 years ago.

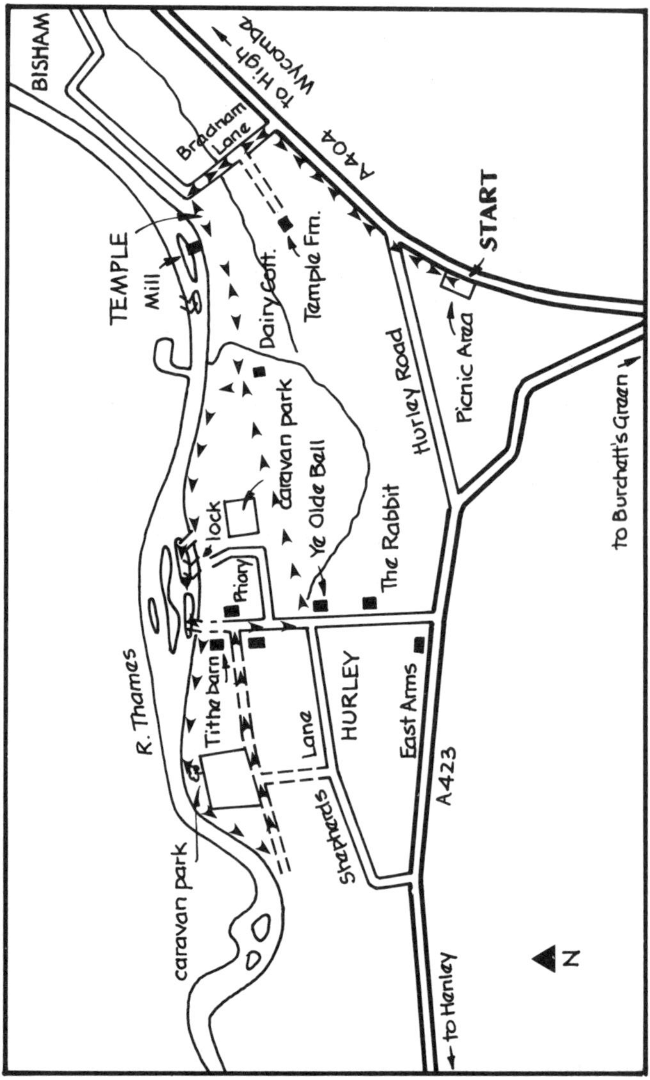
BISHAM
to High Wycombe
Bradnam Lane
A404
START
TEMPLE
Mill
Dairy Cott.
Temple Fm.
Hurley Road
Picnic Area
Caravan park
Ye Olde Bell
The Rabbit
lock
Priory
to Burchett's Green
R. Thames
Tithe barn
Lane
HURLEY
East Arms
A423
Shepherds
caravan park
to Henley
N

WALK SEVEN

The Thames at Hurley

Introduction: No roads go through Hurley. Two quiet lanes go into the village and lead back out the same way. It is, therefore, a peaceful and beautifully unspoilt village that is a delight to explore on foot. The remains of Ladye Place and a Benedictine priory; the parish church; ancient barns and a dovecot together with Ye Olde Bell will all appeal to lovers of history and ancient buildings. This walk goes through the village whilst making a six-mile circuit of the level Thames Valley meadowland that surrounds it. The way goes through Temple and alongside the shortest reach between locks on the Thames. It makes use of an island to get by Hurley Lock and there are attractive views of the hanging woods on the Buckinghamshire bank. The route is easily followed and without hills except for one gentle climb near the end.

Distance: 6 miles of which 2¾ miles are on made-up surfaces. An optional cut, pointed out at the appropriate place in the text, reduces the distance to 4½ miles. The full route takes about 2½ hours without stops or detours.

Refreshments: The Rabbit (called The Rising Sun until 1982) in Hurley offers sandwiches and light meals in the bar every day except Sunday evenings.

How to get there: The walk begins and ends at a public picnic site beside the A.404 between the Burchett's Green and Bisham roundabouts. At the Burchett's Green roundabout, where the A.423 and A.404 cross, follow the A.404 in the direction of Marlow and High Wycombe. The lay-by and picnic site are on the left-hand side ¾ mile from the roundabout. This section of the A.404 is a

WALK SEVEN

dual carriageway so, if coming from the opposite direction, it is still necessary to go up to the Burchett's Green roundabout and then to come back down the correct carriageway.

The walk: Leave the picnic area and walk alongside the A.404 in the direction of Marlow. After 600 yards turn into quiet Bradnam Lane. It goes off to the left and is signposted to Temple ½ mile. Bradnam Lane goes down to the level floor of the Thames Valley and heads towards a group of white-walled houses. The tight huddle of buildings of Temple Farm are over to the left whilst a long field-width to the right is a healing spring called Princess Elizabeth's Well (see notes). A little over a ½ mile from the main road the lane comes to a 'T' junction among the houses at Temple.

Turn left and follow the road for 100 yards to the point where it swings sharp right towards Temple Mills. Go straight on here. Ignore the "No Through Road" sign; it is for vehicles. Within a few yards the road reduces to a footpath that goes on alongside a brick wall that surrounds Temple Weir House. You may hear the sound of tumbling water from the weir as you go along here. The path goes through a brick-sided tunnel barely high enough to stand in, and then joins a hard surfaced track. Continue along this track. It meanders attractively between trees and, in places, it becomes a raised causeway across a swamp. Passing a pumping station on the left, the path then goes through a little wrought-iron gate and onto a tarmac drive that serves white-painted Dairy Cottage over to the left.

A dozen steps on from the wrought-iron gate a footpath goes off to the right. It is signposted to the river. Go over a concrete stile and follow the path for 200 yards to the Thames where it arrives under the spreading branches of a huge horse chestnut tree. There is a large marina at the opposite bank, and Temple Lock and weirs are just in view downstream.

Turn left and walk upstream beside the river. Very soon the route goes across a pleasant level meadow dotted with trees. A little over ¼ mile upstream there is a group of islands in the river. There is a beautiful view between two of them over to red-brick Harleyford Manor, set above terraced lawns on the far bank.

The path then turns to the right and goes over a high arched footbridge onto one of the islands. The route continues its upstream direction by going along the island. Across the channel to the left is Peter Freebody's 300-year-old boat-building busi-

THE THAMES AT HURLEY

ness. Its craftsmen still build and repair boats with mahogany planking fastened together with copper rivets that gleam through thick coats of varnish. Continue past Hurley Lock to the upstream tip of the island. There, another high footbridge returns the path to the Berkshire bank where the forward footpath goes away from the river and into Hurley village. The walk can be shortened by 1½ miles by going straight into Hurley instead of following the next section.

To continue the full route, turn right when you step off the bridge and walk upstream beside the river. The path goes over another footbridge in front of a riverside house and then out into popular Thames-side meadows. There are weirs over to the right and a caravan park a little way off to the left. Behind is an attractive view of Hurley. Go on alongside the river where the right bank is mostly wooded and has high white chalk cliffs facing this way.

The river curves around to the left and the path goes through a fence from one field to another. 200 yards further on it arrives in front of a cluster of buildings. At the same point a gravel track from the caravan park angles in from the left.

Turn left and cross the gravel track to an iron field gate where a signpost indicates the footpath. It heads back towards Hurley and runs along the edge of the caravan park. 150 yards further on is a crossroads at the entrance to the caravan park. Continue forwards along a gravel road with the caravan park still on your left-hand side. Pleasant level meadows lie to the right. ¾ of a mile brings this road to a 'T' junction in front of a high flint-and-brick wall at the edge of Hurley. Behind the wall is a house converted from a tithe barn and a lovely old dovecot thought to have been built in the 14th century. It is round with buttressed walls and a clay tiled roof (see notes).

Carry straight on, going over a stile and onto a footpath which goes for 75 yards between the flint-and-brick wall and the buildings of Hurley Farm on the right. It then emerges into a car park. Over to the left is the Church of St Mary the Virgin (see notes) whilst nearer and to the right you will see an impressive stone-built barn (see notes).

At the far side of the car park, a road runs from left to right. It comes up from the river where the route earlier came off the island by Hurley Lock. Turn right which will lead you away from the river. Follow the road to a small triangular green overlooked

WALK SEVEN

by the Old Vicarage on the right. Go straight on between attractive old village houses, the Post Office and Church House (see notes), to a junction where Shepherd's Lane goes off to the right. If you continue straight on for 150 yards you will find the Rabbit public house on the left-hand side.

Opposite Shepherd's Lane a footpath goes off to the left. It is signed and leaves the road immediately before arriving in front of Ye Olde Bell, a beautiful old inn built 850 years ago (see notes). Turn into this path. It goes between high fences and leads away from the village and out into open countryside once more. After a few minutes walk you will arrive at a little tarmac road.

Continue the forward direction over a cattle grid and onto the road. There is another caravan park across to the left. 600 yards on from the cattle grid the road turns sharply to the right and runs towards a solitary white-walled house. Suddenly you recognise it as Dairy Cottage, passed on the outward route. Do not go round towards Dairy Cottage but keep going straight on. A few steps will take you through a familiar wrought-iron gate and onto the footpath used earlier. Follow the footpath back along the outward route. Go by the swampy section and through the tunnel to Temple. Turn right in Temple and follow Bradnam Lane up to the dual carriageway A.404 with the lofty beech trees of Bradnam Wood beyond. Turn right at the main road and go back alongside it for 600 yards to the picnic site where the walk started.

Hurley - Historical Notes

Princess Elizabeth's Well: This is a freshwater spring that for centuries was thought to have magical healing powers. The water was said to be of special benefit to the eyes. Even up to the end of the 19th century it was believed that if the water was splashed on the face it would cure afflictions of the eye and improve vision.

Harleyford Manor: The Manor was shown on the first Ordnance Survey maps as "Hurleyford Manor". This name implies that there used to be a ford here that crossed the river to Hurley.

Church of St. Mary the Virgin, Hurley: There has been a church at Hurley since Saxon times: probably from around 600 AD. The present building still has part Saxon walls and clear traces of Norman and later work. (Some of the Norman style stonework dates only from a mid-nineteenth century restoration.) The village church was endowed as a Benedictine Priory by Geoffrey de Mandeville and dedicated in 1086 by Bishop Osmund (later St Osmund the Good) of Salisbury. The priory buildings expanded and the present St Mary's was then just the nave of its church. In 1536 Hurley Priory, together with most of the lesser monasteries in the country, was suppressed by Henry VIII. The buildings were disposed of and the church reverted to its orginal role of village church. Among many items of interest within the church is a painted monument to the Lovelace family on the north wall of the sanctuary. It has been there for about 400 years but its lower part is hidden from view because of a later raising of the floor level.

Hurley Priory: A Benedictine priory was founded at Hurley in the year of the Domesday survey, 1086. St Mary's is a remaining part of the priory church which was then much larger. It extended 120 feet further eastwards and had side aisles and chapels. The foundations of some of its outer walls still exist in the grounds of the house called "Cloisters". On the north side of the church (the side nearest the river) a stone archway leads through to an attractive quadrangle which was the original quadrangle of the priory. It is private property and bounded by houses that incorporate remains of the priory buildings. The wall of the house opposite the church was originally the south wall of the refectory where the monks ate. The priory stood in grounds of 20 acres and there is plenty of evidence to show how it must have looked during its 450 years existence. It was suppressed along with other small monastic foundations in the first enforcements of the Dissolution in 1536.

Dovecote: A very good example of a medieval dovecote dating from about 1300. It was then a privilege for lords of the manor to be allowed to keep pigeons. The birds and their eggs were a valuable source of food in the days before farm animals could be kept in numbers through the winter. This dovecote has spaces for 750 nesting pairs.

The Tithe Barn: A lovely old barn of about the same date as the dovecote. It was converted to a fine house in 1950.

The Old Priory Barn: Beside the road by the public car park, this

WALK SEVEN

impressive barn is thought to be even older than the tithe barn. It is built of flint and clunch (chalk blocks) and is very attractive. It still gives good service as a farm barn after seven centuries of use.

Ladye Place: This fine Tudor mansion was built on the land of Hurley Priory about ten years after its dissolution. It was built by John Lovelace who died in 1558 and whose tomb can be seen in the sanctuary of the church. The mansion was built over the old priory crypt which then served as its cellar. In 1688 the third Lord Lovelace of Hurley held clandestine meetings in that cellar at which was hatched the plot to overthrow Catholic King James II by inviting his Protestant nephew, William of Orange, to bring a force from Holland to seize the throne of England. After the successful carrying through of the plot, William, by then King William III, came to Ladye Place to see where the revolution had begun. The mansion was pulled down in 1837. The only part that remains today is a small section of its front that is embodied in the churchyard wall, and some stately cedar trees that once graced its grounds.

Hurley Post Office: This is accommodated in one of three refurbished 18th century almshouses.

Church House: It dates from the 14th century and has seen service as a workhouse and as parish rooms, but has now been sold to a private owner.

Ye Olde Bell: A beautiful black and white half-timbered inn in the middle of Hurley. There is a wooden settle against the front wall and a board, fixed high up, which states it was built in 1135. It originated as a hospice attached to Hurley Priory; a place where the monks accommodated weary travellers. An underground passage runs from the inn to the former crypt of the priory.

WALK EIGHT

Wokingham to Crowthorne via Gorrick Plantation

Introduction: This is a longish figure-of-eight route that goes from Wokingham to Crowthorne and back. For those who prefer less lengthy routes it can be cut quite conveniently into shorter walks. For instance, the outward route from Wokingham can be walked and the return made by train from Crowthorne Station. Similarly the return half of the route can be enjoyed on another occasion. Alternatively, each of the two circles that make up the figure eight can be walked as separate 4¼ mile roundwalks. The route takes in farmland, pine plantations, heathland, ponds, a golf course and a little bit of urban Wokingham. It provides a very pleasant walk through varied scenery.

Distance: 8½ miles. (or four different 4¼ miles walks as mentioned above.)

Refreshments: The Who'datho'tit, Nine Mile Ride serves snacks and light meals at lunch times except on Sundays. The pies are all home-made. The outward and return routes both pass within a few hundred yards of this pub.

How to get there: Start from Wokingham Station, easily found near the town centre and with parking space nearby. If walking part of the route only, and starting in Crowthorne, begin at Crowthorne Station. It is beside the A.3095 road to Finchampstead at the western outskirts of Crowthorne. There is adequate car parking space here too. Trains run between the 2 stations at hourly intervals during the day from Monday to Saturday. On Sunday an approximately 2-hourly service operates. Crowthorne station is unmanned, and passengers pay the conductor on the train.

WALK EIGHT

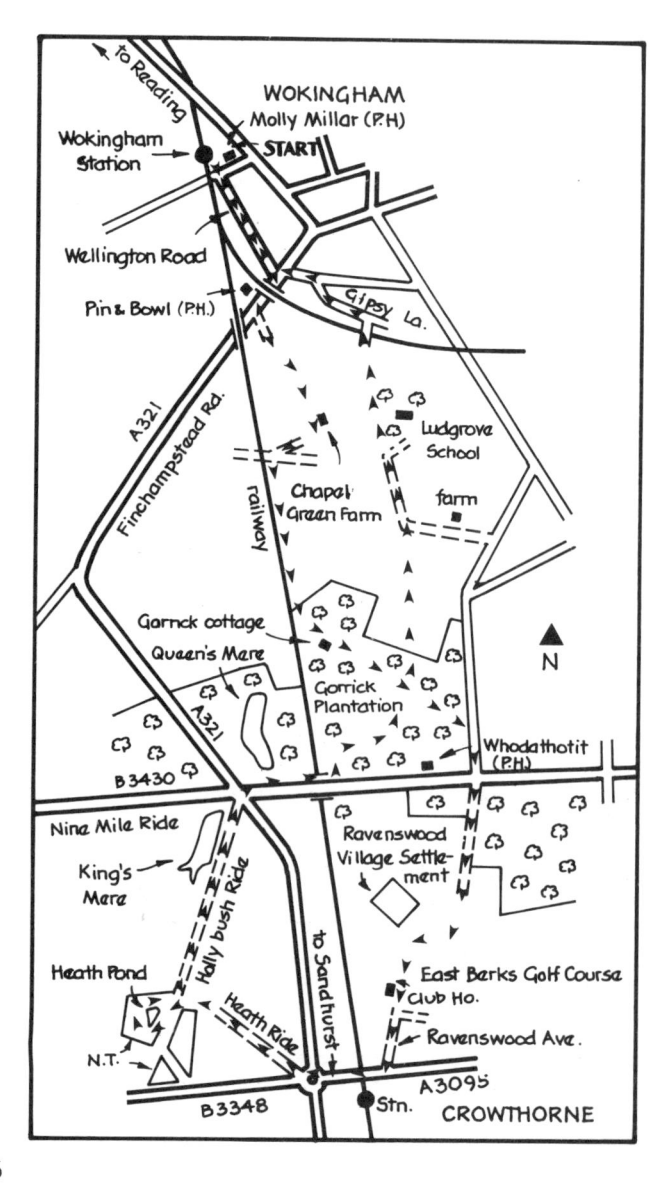

The walk: Leave Wokingham station on the town (West) side of the track. With the Molly Millar public house on your left and a level crossing on your right, cross the main road. Go into Wellington Road and follow it to its junction with Finchampstead Road. Turn right here and follow the main road down and under a brick-arched railway bridge. Pass the low, white-walled Pin and Bowl on the right-hand side and then go over a little stream. 20 yards past the stream turn left, away from the main road. A firm drive with hedges alongside takes you to the entrance to Wokingham Equestrain Centre. Keep going along the drive which now has paddocks with horses in them alongside. The drive arrives at a cross-tracks amid stables and paddocks. Follow it round to the right and keep to it as it follows a straight line between paddocks; fences bordering. After a few moments the path spills onto a broad drive. It continues ahead, passes a house, and then runs by the high garden wall of Chapel Green Farm. Notice the small antique bricks used in this wall. After 160 yards the drive turns sharply to the right. The entrance to Chapel Green Farm is on the left and there is a good view of the lovely old building from here. It is a large house of two storeys and shaped, in plan, like a letter 'E' without the centre bar. Above the main door is an inscribed stone tablet and a large central gable. Above the gable is a lantern structure topped by a windvane bearing the date 1665 in large gold figures.

Follow the drive around to the right and head away from Chapel Green Farm. After 100 yards it angles around to the left and meets another drive. Cross straight over it and follow a straight drive with a band of trees along the right-hand side. Behind the trees is the Wokingham to Crowthorne railway line. The drive continues straight and more-or-less level for ¾ mile. There are attractive open farmland views to the left but the views to the right are mostly cut short by trees. Eventually the drive curves around to the left. It goes through a wooden gate with a stile beside it and enters a birch wood. The drive then crosses a stream and goes up a short slope to some barns and an old farmhouse in a clearing. This is Gorrick Cottage, now renovated and enlarged.

Sixty yards past Gorrick Cottage the track again enters woods by a wooden gate. This time you will notice that, instead of natural mixed woodland, the wood to the right of the track is a plantation of conifers. It is Gorrick Plantation, part of Bramshill Forest,

WALK EIGHT

owned and managed by the Forestry Commission. Keep going forward. There are now plantations on both sides. 600 yards after entering Gorrick Wood the way comes to a cross-tracks among the trees. Here is where the return route crosses the outward route. Continue straight over this cross-tracks and within another 600 yards the track will take you out of the Forestry Commission's plantation and onto Heathlands Road. Turn right along this motor road and follow it for 600 yards to a 'T' junction where it meets Nine Mile Ride (see notes).

The route goes straight on but a short detour here will take you to the Who'datho'tit; a pub 300 yards along the Nine Mile Ride to the right. Return to the Heathlands Road junction and go straight over Nine Mile Ride into an entrance drive with commemorative gates. It leads to Ravenswood Village Settlement and there is a right-of-way along it for walkers. The drive leads directly to former Ravenswood Farm and swings sharply to the right towards the modern buildings of the Village Settlement. Do not follow it around to the right, but maintain the same forward direction.

A track goes along the left-hand side of the group of buildings and then curves around behind them. Follow it until clear of the buildings. It then becomes a narrower, but still well-defined, footpath. Follow this footpath for 100 yards to a 'T' junction where it meets another path at the edge of East Berks. Golf Course. Turn right and follow this path for 150 yards. It goes by a large house on the right to a junction with a private small tarmac drive that leads into Ravenswood Village Settlement from the Crowthorne direction.

Turn left at this point and follow the drive across the golf course. Go through a spinney that encloses a pair of houses and then go by the club house and golf club car parks, continuing forwards. The drive becomes a road, called Ravenswood Avenue, and has modern houses alongside. A quarter of a mile from the golf course it emerges onto Duke's Ride in Crowthorne (A.3095). Turn right along Duke's Ride which will take you to Crowthorne Station 150 yards along on the left. There is a choice of return routes from here. Either return to Wokingham Station by train, walk back the way you came or walk back by the alternative route which follows.

Leave Crowthorne Station and turn left along Duke's Ride. Follow it for 150 yards, with houses on the right and playing fields on the left, to a roundabout where the A321 crosses. Straight ahead is Wellingtonia Avenue, a straight road between two magnificent ranks of wellingtonia firs that rise towards Finchampstead Ridges (see notes).

Heath Ride leaves the roundabout just to the right of Wellingtonia Avenue and is the route to take. It is a pot-holed track that serves the houses dotted among the trees. It goes firstly through mixed woodland with lots of chestnut trees and then rises between conifer plantations. There is a good chance of hearing woodpeckers or seeing the blue and white flash of a jay as you go through here. At the top of the rise there is a cross-tracks. Turn left onto a lesser track that goes alongside the high garden wall of a house called "Hermitage". Soon there is a pinewood along the left-hand side. Called Simons Wood, it is fringed with rhododendron bushes and is owned by the National Trust. To the right of the path is heathland; all birch and bracken and very attractive.

The path descends to a cross-tracks where the route turns to the right. Do not immediately take this turning. Ahead, in the angle formed between the forward and left-hand tracks, is Heath Pond; a lovely sheet of water surrounded by trees and sandy banks. The lake and its immediate surroundings are owned by the National Trust and always open to visitors. A stroll around it is well worthwhile. It takes about 20 minutes to walk from Crowthorne Station to Heath Pond.

Return to the cross-tracks and take the direction away from the pond that was indicated earlier (N.E.). The track is straight. After 200 yards or so it acquires houses alongside and further along, boasts a made-up surface. It is called Hollybush Ride and goes alongside King's Mere, largest of the heathland pools dotted about this district. Its placid surface can be seen through the bushes on the left-hand side. A little over ½ mile from Heath Pond brings Hollybush Ride to a junction where it meets Nine Mile Ride just yards away from the point where it is crossed by the A.321 Wokingham to Sandhurst road.

Turn right here. Cross the A.321 and go along Nine Mile Ride in the direction signed towards Bracknell. Cross a tiny stream that feeds Queen's Mere, hidden among the trees to the left. Follow the slope and go over a high-humped railway bridge. 120 yards past the bridge turn left onto a footpath that leaves the road immediately before the houses begin on that side. (You could visit the Who'datho'tit from here by going straight on along Nine Mile Ride for ¼ mile. It is then on the left.

WALK EIGHT

The path that goes away from Nine Mile Ride follows a drive that leads to a gated entrance to Gorrick Wood. Go forward into the plantation. Follow a broad track for 200 yards to a point where it divides into three. Take the track that angles away to the right. At the next cross-tracks turn left and walk for 250 yards to a junction at the top of a rise. Ignore the two tracks that go off to the left and the one to the right. Continue straight ahead for another 200 yards to yet another cross-tracks. Go straight on and follow a lesser track, still between trees. This track soon reduces to a footpath and descends to cross a little stream by a footbridge made from split logs. The ground around here can sometimes be muddy. A few yards past the footbridge, and only three minutes from the last cross-tracks, the path comes to the edge of the wood.

Continue forwards. Go away from the wood and across open fields. Within 100 yards the path comes to a cross-tracks where the forward way becomes a firm farm track. Ignore the right-hand track and continue along it between open vegetable fields with neither fences nor hedges. Gorrick Wood now lies well back to the left whilst one field-width to the right, Heathlands Road is hidden in a band of trees. The track continues straight and level. A wood fills the forward horizon and above it the distant spire of Wokingham Church protrudes.

The track goes by a sports field on the left and then swings sharply to the right in front of a wood. There is no right-of-way along that track. A footpath maintains the forward direction by going along the extreme left-hand side of the wood. It can be rather hidden but is well-used and straight. For 350 yards it has the wooded grounds of Ludgrove School on its right until an iron kissing gate lets it out onto a quiet tarmac road. It is the same road that was crossed near Chapel Green Farm on the outward section of the walk. In fact Chapel Green Farm can be seen from here. It is about 350 yards away to the left on a little rise.

Go straight across the tarmac road. Another iron kissing gate lets you through to a hard drive that continues the line of the walk. After crossing a swift-flowing stream among trees the way begins a gentle rise, and is soon in the open once more. Wokingham Equestrian Centre is only a short way off to the left and most of the fields hereabouts have horses in them. Ahead there are now glimpses of the outermost houses of Wokingham. Stay with the path until it arrives at a high concrete footbridge that takes it over the Wokingham to Bracknell railway line. A short path goes from the other side of the bridge, between houses, to Gipsy Lane.

Turn left along this urban road and, after 30 yards, bear left alongside Langborough Recreation Ground. Continue along Gipsy Lane to its junction with Langborough Road. Turn left here and after 60 yards turn left again into Finchampstead Road. 60 yards along Finchampstead Road brings you to a junction with Wellington Road. Turn right here and retrace your steps along Wellington Road to the station where the walk commenced.

Wokingham to Crowthorne - Historical Notes

Nine Mile Ride: This was made on the instructions of George III who reigned 1760-1810. It was cut through what was then still part of Windsor Forest and a royal hunting preserve. The present motor road still follows the straight line of the original forest ride.

Wellingtonia Avenue: A beautiful avenue between two straight lines of impressive wellingtonia trees. The road was made and the trees planted by John Walter III of Bearwood Park. It was opened to the public in 1863. Wellingtonias originate in California where they are commonly known as "big tree" or "mammoth tree". They were introduced in to this country in 1853 and were named after the first Duke of Wellington, a popular national hero who had died the year before.

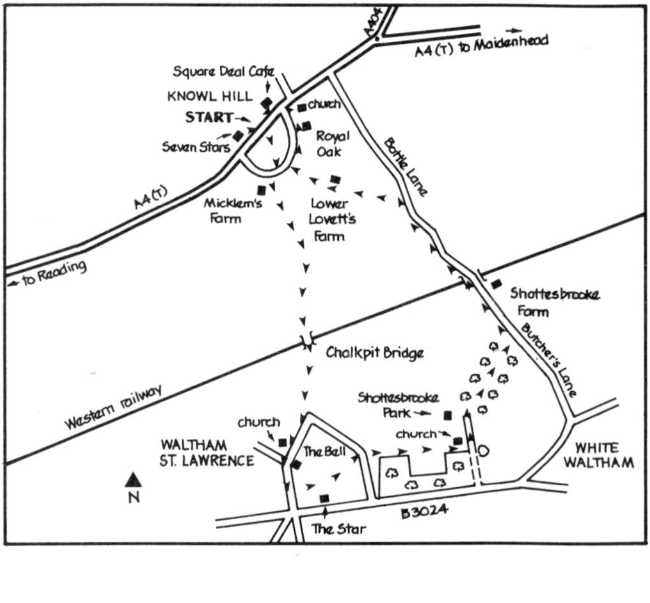
A404
A4 (T) to Maidenhead
Square Deal Cafe
KNOWL HILL
START
church
Seven Stars
Royal Oak
A4(T)
Micklem's Farm
Lower Lovett's Farm
Bottle Lane
to Reading
Shottesbrooke Farm
Butcher's Lane
Chalkpit Bridge
Western railway
Shottesbrooke Park
church
church
WALTHAM ST. LAWRENCE
The Bell
WHITE WALTHAM
N
B3024
The Star

WALK NINE

Knowl Hill
and Waltham St. Lawrence

Introduction: This walk makes a circuit over the level farming countryside to the west of Maidenhead. The paths are all well used and reasonably easy to follow. In spring this walk is enriched by an abundance of wild flowers and blossom and their scents. Part of the way goes along quiet country lanes that are beautifully rural. It goes through the villages of Knowl Hill and Waltham St. Lawrence. At Shottesbrooke it visits an outstanding medieval church and goes close by the house at Shottesbrooke Park.

Distance: This walk is 5½ miles long and takes about 3 hours including time spent visiting churches etc. along the way.

Refreshments: At the start The Seven Stars always has rolls and toasted sandwiches on offer. The Bird in Hand, 500 yards along the A.4 towards Reading, serves meals of excellent value. The Square Deal transport cafe, also close to the start, serves snacks and meals until 3.30pm each weekday. At Waltham St. Lawrence snacks and light meals are served in the bar of The Bell at lunchtimes from Monday to Saturday.

How to get there: Start at Knowl Hill, a village 4½ miles west of Maidenhead on the A.4 road towards Reading. Alder Valley buses drop their passengers on the A.4 and cars can be parked in a service road beside the main dual-carriageway. The service road is on the north side of the A.4. It has the Square Deal Cafe at its Maidenhead end and The Seven Stars public house at the other.

The walk: Leave the service road at the end by the Square Deal Cafe. Cross the dual-carriageway A.4 and walk for a few yards in

WALK NINE

the direction of Maidenhead. Turn right onto a footpath that climbs a grassy slope that goes away from the road. This is Knowl Hill Common. It is a beautiful open space; rich in wild flowers and blossom during spring and summer. Climb to the top of the slope where there is a seat cut from a solid tree trunk. There are lovely views both backwards and forwards from here. Behind and below, the brown roofs of Knowl Hill nestle in a cosy hollow with Ashley Hill rising to the rear. Looking forwards there are very far-reaching views over a low level farming landscape. You can see White Waltham Airfield half left and Windsor Castle in a straight line beyond. Ahead, looking over the roofs of Knowl Hill Farm, rectangular high-rise buildings give away the position of distant Bracknell. This forward view overlooks the area through which the rest of the walk will go.

Continue the walk by following the path that angles down to the right. It joins a hard drive and goes on down to meet the little road that runs along the far edge of the common. Turn right for 100 yards along this road and then turn left into a narrow drive signed to Micklem's Farmhouse. Go along this short drive. The farmhouse and barns lie over to the right. Keep straight on, following a bush-lined track that heads out over the level landscape. After ⅓ mile the track comes to a junction where another path from Knowl Hill comes in from the left. Veer to the right and continue the direction taken so far. The hedges and trees alongside the track get bigger until they meet overhead. The path is still quite clear and goes on through this attractive tunnel, lined either with leafy or bare branches depending on the season.

A little over ½ mile from the last junction of paths, the way comes to Chalkpit Bridge. A level iron bridge carries the track over the main railway line from Reading to Bristol. The path continues for half a mile along field edges with a hedge on its left-hand side. It then arrives at a by-lane with a tarmac surface. Turn right and proceed along this lane for 100 yards to a 'T' junction and there turn right. Walk along the pretty village road for a little over ¼ mile to Waltham St Lawrence Church (see notes). The church is on the right. It has walls of flint and, in the churchyard, there is an enormous yew tree (see notes). At the entrance is a lych gate with two wooden benches sheltered beneath its roof. The road widens outside the churchyard gate. In the centre of the open area there is a grassy island with a railed enclosure. This is the old village pound where straying animals were put until reclaimed by their owners. Across to the left is a beautiful timber-framed inn: The Bell. (see notes). With the pound behind you and The Bell to your left continue the walk through the village. Pass the Post Office Stores and, opposite Paradise Cottages, turn left onto a footpath.

The path goes away from the road and alongside some allotment gardens. Where the allotments end go over a stile and angle left across a paddock. Cross another stile and angle right to yet another. Go over the field ahead to its far corner where a stile lets you out on to a country road opposite an isolated pair of houses. Go straight over the road. A signed footpath continues the forward direction along the left-hand side of the houses. 100 yards from the road it arrives at the corner of Burringham Wood, an extensive stand of huge sycamores. Continue along the edge of the wood. There is open farmland to the left and the view reaches to Ashley Hill, one of the most prominent landmarks in East Berkshire. The path follows several twists and turns but stays always along the edge of the wood.

At the end of the wood go over a stile and forward across a meadow to a wooden kissing gate at the far side. The well-kept grounds and buildings of Shottesbrooke Park lie across to the left. The path goes straight on, under a low brick bridge and between high garden walls until it arrives unexpectedly in front of Shottesbrooke Church (see notes). Continue walking in the same direction after having visited the church. Go first through a pair of oak gates and then through an iron kissing gate to a small tarmac road. Across the road there is a broad grassy area and to the right a large pond. Turn left and follow the road, passing in front of Shottesbrooke Park (see notes).

Do not follow the road round when it swings towards the house but carry straight on along a grassy track at the edge of a meadow. After 100 yards the track veers to the right and goes through a long impressive avenue of stately old lime trees. At the end of the avenue go over a stile to a motor road. There is an unusual lodge here; the sides facing the track and the road are built to look like a chapel. Turn left along the road which is called Butchers Lane. The big white buildings at White Waltham Airfield can be picked out over the fields to the right. A short distance along Butchers Lane will take you past Shottesbrooke Farm to a bridge over the London to Bristol railway line. There is a very pleasant view from

WALK NINE

the bridge. It ranges over a neatly farmed landscape with scarcely a tree or building in sight except in the distance. Bowsey Hill rises at the forward horizon. Interestingly, local weather lore says "When Bowsey Hill begins to smoke, Shottesbrooke will get a soak".

Continue for ½ mile along the road which has now changed its name to Bottle Lane. It turns sharply to the right around the first house that it comes to. Leave the road 100 yards past the turning. Go onto a signed footpath that leads away on the left-hand side. It follows field edges and, at first, has a hedgerow on its right-hand side. The path then goes on over open fields to an electricity substation. Follow the footpath along the right-hand side of this installation and around the back of it to where it joins a track. The track goes forward for 200 yards and then turns to the right. It goes by the boarded black barns of Lower Lovetts Farm and gains a tarmac surface. It then rises for 200 yards to join the little road that skirts Knowl Hill Common.

The shortest way back to the point where the walk began is straight ahead, up and over the common to the A.4. Alternatively, turn right and follow the road for 300 yards to The Royal Oak public house. After another 100 yards you will pass St. Peter's, a brick walled church built in 1841. At the A.4. turn left and the service road where the walk began will be found 200 yards along on the opposite side.

Knowl Hill and Waltham St. Lawrence - Historical Notes

Church of St. Laurence at Waltham St. Lawrence: This is a very large village church with an aisle each side of the nave. The oldest parts of the building are the walls of the nave. They date from the 11th century and probably formed part of an earlier church. St. Laurence's was extended early in the 14th century at which time it gained its tower. The tower was increased in height two centuries later and the whole church underwent much restoration in Victorian times.

Yew Tree: The enormous tree in the churchyard is reputed to have been planted in 1635 by Thomas Wilkinson, the then rector.

The Bell Inn: A beautiful 14th century timber-framed building of two storeys. The upper storey overhangs the lower except for a recessed bay in the centre. The neighbouring cottages are almost as old as the inn and together they form a most picturesque group.

Church of St. John the Baptist at Shottesbrooke: This is a superb example of medieval church architecture. It was built about 1337 on the site of an earlier church. Shottesbrooke village was wiped out soon afterwards by the Black Death and the small population of the parish since then had been unable to finance any remodelling of their church during the periods when it was fashionable to do so. The result is a complete example of a relatively rare style of church building. It is cruciform in plan with a central tower topped by a very tall spire. Inside it is plain but light and beautifully proportioned. There are numerous memorials to the local lords of the manor who lived next door at Shottesbrooke Park. Most of the windows contain some medieval glass. Shottesbrooke Church is one of only two collegiate churches in Berkshire. Sir William Trussel, lord of the manor, founded a college at Shottesbrooke and endowed it with this church. The college was later destroyed by fire. There is a legend that the architect of the church died by falling from the top of the spire where he was fixing the weather vane. He is said to have been buried where he fell, under a flat stone that can still be seen outside the church door.

Shottesbrooke Park: Seat of the lords of the manor of Shottesbrooke. The house is part Tudor. It originates from the second half of the 16th century although it looks more recent. It underwent a complete restoration in the 18th century, and the parapet was added in the 19th century. Some 18th and 19th century additions have since been removed. Among other owners have been the Trussell, Cherry and Vansittart families. One, Francis Cherry, was described by Queen Anne as "one of the honestest gentlemen in her dominions". Mr Cherry was an excellent horseman and is reputed to have tried to tempt the "Dutch King" (William III) to his death by jumping his horse into a deep part of the Thames whilst the king was following him closely.

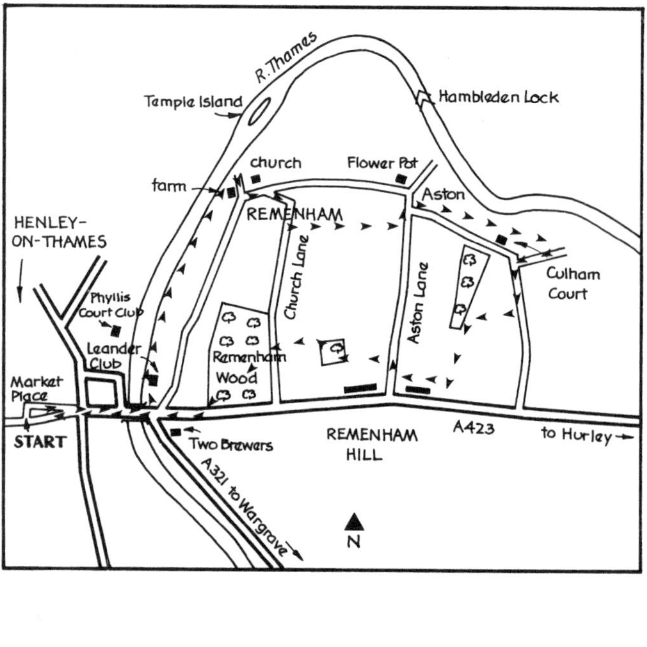
R. Thames
Temple Island
Hambleden Lock
church
Flower Pot
farm
Aston
REMENHAM
HENLEY-
ON-THAMES
Church Lane
Aston Lane
Culham
Court
Phyllis
Court Club
Leander
Club
Remenham
Wood
Market
Place
START
Two Brewers
REMENHAM
HILL
A423
to Hurley
A321 to Wargrave
N

WALK TEN

Henley and Remenham

Introduction: This walk starts and ends in Henley-on-Thames. It crosses the river and circles through a little-known but very lovely corner of Berkshire. This quiet, rural area is bounded on three sides by the Thames and on the south by the Henley to Maidenhead road; the A.432(T). The walk leaves Henley by following the famous regatta course downriver. It then goes through Remenham and by footpath over high rolling countryside to Aston where refreshments can be had "during hours" at The Flower Pot Hotel. The route continues over level farmland before climbing back to Remenham Hill. It then wends its way back to Henley along quiet footpaths that descend through Remenham Wood to the bottom of White Hill less than ½ mile from the much-pictured river bridge that leads back into the town.

Distance: This route is 6 miles long and will take about 3 hours to walk.

Refreshments: There are numerous hotels, pubs and restaurants in Henley. 2½ miles from the start the route goes within 50 yards of The Flower Pot Hotel in Aston which serves sandwiches and light snack meals in the bar.

How to get there: Henley is well served with public transport. Alder Valley buses come from most directions and converge on the Market Place. There is a branch railway connecting with Twyford on the main Paddington to Bristol line. Motorists can leave their cars in either of two car parks close to the Market Place.

The walk: Start from the Market Place in Henley. With your back to the Town Hall go down through the town towards the church.

WALK TEN

Cross the Thames by an old stone bridge to the Berkshire bank. Twenty yards past the bridge take the first turning to the left. Almost immediately there are two footpaths that fork left and right. Take the left-hand path. It winds its way to the riverside and swings around to the right to follow it downstream. The path has a tarmac surface and passes the front of the famous Leander Club (see notes), and then through neat areas of grass where marquees and stands are put up for the Royal Regatta each July (see notes).

The path retains its surface and goes on alongside the stretch of river where the rowing course is staked out each summer for the regattas. Ahead is the ornamental 'temple' on the upstream end of Temple Island (see notes). Pass a short footpath that goes off to the right to Remenham Lane. Go by some attractively converted farmworkers' cottages and the buildings of Remenham Farm 50 yards to the right. Turn right here which will lead you away from the river. Cross a stile beside a farm gate and follow a lane that goes by the farmyard and into the tiny village of Remenham. The lane passes the entrance to Remenham Manor on the left and then brings you to St. Nicholas' Church (see notes) and a 'T' junction. Turn left at the junction, and walk for 100 yards to a fork signed left to Aston and right to Maidenhead. Follow the right fork. It is called Church Lane and climbs in a long right-hand curve. The path goes by a graveyard, a disused chalkpit and through a wood before completing its climb.

100 yards past the wood a gap in the hedge alongside the lane gives access to a footpath that goes off to the left beside a football pitch. It follows a farm track which is a right-of-way for walkers. This path provides superb walking over high undulating farmland. There is a splendid view to the left across the Thames Valley to the wooded hills of South Buckinghamshire. Across the fields to the right are the houses of Remenham Hill. (These will be passed on the return part of the walk). Follow the track for ½ mile until it passes a belt of trees on the right. About 150 yards past the wood it swings sharply to the left and goes down to meet the lane from Remenham to Aston. That downhill stretch is not a public right-of-way. The footpath goes straight on, out of the wood and along field edges. After 250 yards it goes beside Highway Cottage and drops to Aston Lane.

Turn left now and go down the lane for 100 yards to a junction by a timber-built house. The route turns to the right at this junction but if you wish to visit The Flower Pot Hotel it is just 50 yards

HENLEY AND REMENHAM

straight on along Aston Lane. Continue the walk by going from the timber house along the lane signed to Culham Court and Holme Farm. The lane goes above the farm and then turns sharply right. Do not follow it round but go straight on. The route goes over 25 yards of grass to a fence and an iron gate. Go through the iron gate and take a few steps to the left. The footpath then resumes the forward direction. It goes along a bank that separates small fields. Pass an isolated clump of trees and keep on to the gardens of Culham Court (see notes). The large house stands above you to the right, whilst to the left the Thames glints up from below. Go on along the edge of Culham Court's garden with its iron railings on your right. An iron gate lets you through a crossing fence where lawns sweep down to the river. Go straight across the lawns and out through another gate at the far side. Maintain the same forward direction over the next field. White painted arrows on fence posts confirm the route. Leave the field at the far side and go out to a stony drive that curves towards an isolated group of houses over to the left.

Turn right and go along the track for 250 yards to a 'T' junction. Turn left and go uphill for another 250 yards. Pass the entrance drive to Culham House and go on to a small clump of beech trees. Leave the track here. Take to a footpath that goes off to the right. It follows field edges down through a broad hollow and up the other side to a wood. Turn left and go alongside the wood. The path continues to rise and there are superb views back over the Thames Valley. When the wood ends, continue ahead with a hedge on your right-hand side. 30 yards past the wood a white arrow painted on a concrete post shows where the route switches to the other side of the hedge. Continue in the same direction over high, level farmland towards the row of houses that can be seen ahead at Remenham Hill.

When level with the back gardens of these houses a path goes off to the right and runs past the back of them for 400 yards to Aston Lane. If you have difficulty in finding this path, go straight on to the main road that runs in front of the houses. Turn right and go along the main road to its junction with Aston Lane. Turn right and go down the lane for 250 yards. Opposite the last of a row of houses on the right, turn left onto a footpath. It goes away from the road for 200 yards among bushes and trees, and then becomes a stony drive near a white-walled house in a hollow to the left. The drive goes for another 120 yards to a junction with a gated drive

WALK TEN

which comes in from the right. Turn right at this point and follow a signed footpath that goes alongside the private drive. It meanders attractively for 350 yards through a tract of open woodland. At the far side a wooden gate lets you out into the open once more. Turn left here and go along a field edge towards two houses nestling under the edge of another wood 300 yards away. Across a meadow to the left is creamy brick Remenham Place whilst to the right the view extends to the beautiful wooded hills around Fawley beyond the Thames.

When the path nears the two houses under the wood it spills out onto quiet Church Lane which, to the right, leads down into Remenham. Angle left across the road and take to a footpath that goes off to the right beside the entrance to Whitewood House. The path is immediately engulfed by Remenham Wood. It is quite narrow but not difficult to follow. It goes straight over a gravel track and on through the trees, and then begins to go downhill. Go between old iron railings to the entrance to a house called Underwood. Continue ahead, now beside a wire strand fence to the point where steps go down beside the entrance to Craigwell House to a main road.

The road is White Hill, a section of the road from Henley to Maidenhead. Turn right and follow it downhill. ¼ mile brings it to a junction where the road to Wargrave and Twyford goes off to the left. In the angle is The Two Brewers from whose stables carters used to be able to hire extra horses to haul their waggons to the top of White Hill. A further 250 yards takes you along the main road to Henley Bridge from where it is a short distance into Henley Market Place where the walk began.

Henley - Historical Notes

Leander Club: Leander is the oldest and most influential of Thames rowing clubs. Its date of origin is unknown but is generally accepted as being in 1818; that is well before the first Oxford and Cambridge University boat race. Leander members are easily spotted during regatta week. They wear pink caps and socks as they watch the races or circulate in the town.

Henley Royal Regatta: Regattas began in Henley a century and a half ago. The first Oxford and Cambridge University boat race took place here on the evening of June 10th, 1829. Ten years later the first Henley Regatta took place. It became a popular annual event offering attractive prizes to successful oarsmen. In 1851 the patronage of Prince Albert, husband of Queen Victoria, gained it the "Royal" title that it still retains. By the end of the 19th century Henley Royal Regatta had become one of the highlights of the English social season. It is still a major social occasion as well as an international competition that draws oarsmen and women from all over the world for the four-day event held in July. The race are rowed over a dead straight course 1 mile 550 yards long. The course has also been used for olympic competitions when the games were held in this country.

Temple Island: The "temple" that gives this island its name is an attractive landscape ornament of the type once fashionable in the gardens of the great houses of England. This one was designed by James Wyatt in 1771 for the grounds of Fawley Court on the other bank of the Thames. The island has sometimes been known as Regatta Island because it marks the start of the regatta course.

St. Nicholas' Church Remenham: There has been a church here at least since Norman times. Parts of the present building seem to date from the twelfth or thirteenth centuries but enthusiastic Victorian restoration work has made them difficult to identify. Within the church are monuments dating from the sixteenth and seventeenth centuries.

Culham Court: An impressive and elegant 18th century house of red brick. It was built 1770-71 for Robert Mitchel.